The North American Fourth Edition

# Cambridge Latin Course

## Unit 1

## Omnibus Workbook

REVISION TEAM

**Stephanie Pope, Chair**
*Norfolk Academy, Norfolk, Virginia*

**Patricia E. Bell**
*Centennial Collegiate and Vocational Institute, Guelph, Ontario, Canada*

**Stan Farrow**
*Formerly of the David and Mary Thomson Collegiate Institute, Scarborough, Ontario, Canada*

**Richard M. Popeck**
*Stuarts Draft High School, Stuarts Draft, Virginia*

**Anne Shaw**
*Lawrence High School and Lawrence Free State High School, Lawrence, Kansas*

CAMBRIDGE
UNIVERSITY PRESS

CAMBRIDGE UNIVERSITY PRESS
Cambridge, New York, Melbourne, Madrid, Cape Town, Singapore,
São Paulo, Delhi, Dubai, Tokyo, Mexico City

Cambridge University Press
32 Avenue of the Americas, New York, NY 10013–2473, USA

www.cambridge.org
Information on this title: www.cambridge.org/9780521787475

The *Cambridge Latin Course* is an outcome of work jointly commissioned by
the Schools Council before its closure and the Cambridge School Classics Project,
and is published under the aegis of Qualifications and Curriculum Authority
Enterprises Limited in London and the North American Cambridge Classics Project.

First published 1983
Third edition 1988
Fourth edition 2001
16th printing 2010

Printed in the United States of America

*A catalog record for this publication is available from the British Library.*

ISBN 978-0-521-78747-5 paperback

Cambridge University Press has no responsibility for the persistence or
accuracy of URLs for external or third-party Internet Web sites referred to in
this publication and does not guarantee that any content on such Web sites is,
or will remain, accurate or appropriate. Information regarding prices, travel
timetables, and other factual information given in this work are correct at
the time of first printing. Cambridge University Press does not guarantee
the accuracy of such information thereafter.

Layout by Newton Harris Design Partnership
Illustrations: Peter Kesteven, Leslie Jones, Joy Mellor, and Neil Sutton

# Preface

This workbook is designed to be used in conjunction with Unit 1 of the **Cambridge Latin Course**. A variety of exercises is provided for each Stage:

- exercises consolidating Latin vocabulary and grammar;
- language awareness exercises, mainly involving work on Latin derivations in English and other modern languages;
- exercises testing oral and/or aural comprehension;
- exercises extending and testing knowledge of the Pompeian setting;
- focused questions on each cultural section.

The *Key to the Omnibus Workbook* can be found in the Unit 1 *Teacher's Manual* (North American Fourth Edition).

This *Omnibus Workbook* is a selection of worksheets from the North American **Cambridge Latin Course** Unit 1 *Workbook* (editors Ed Phinney and Patricia Bell) and the **Cambridge Latin Course** Book 1 *Worksheet Masters* (Cambridge School Classics Project), as well as new material created for the Fourth Edition.

We would like to acknowledge the generosity of the many teachers who willingly shared their ideas and worksheets with us. Of special help with the oral/aural component was Randy Thompson, Churchill High School, San Antonio, Texas, who wrote the *Audīte/Dīcite* exercises.

Lastly we should like to express our indebtedness to Jeni Wetmore, for typing, and Fiona Kelly, our editor, for her expertise, patience, and hard work.

Patricia Bell
Stan Farrow
Stephanie Pope
Richard Popeck
Anne Shaw

# What does he say? What does he do?

*Find the answer to each question by filling the blanks with Latin words which translate the English. Then read the boxed letters downwards.*

1  What does Grumio say?

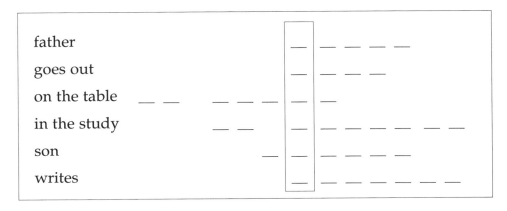

| | |
|---|---|
| father | _ _ _ _ _ |
| goes out | _ _ _ _ |
| on the table | _ _ _ _ _ _ _ |
| in the study | _ _ _ _ _ _ _ _ |
| son | _ _ _ _ _ _ |
| writes | _ _ _ _ _ _ _ |

2  What does Cerberus do?

| | |
|---|---|
| works | _ _ _ _ _ _ _ |
| stands | _ _ _ _ |
| sleeps | _ _ _ _ _ _ |
| enters | _ _ _ _ _ _ |
| shouts | _ _ _ _ _ _ |
| in the garden | _ _ _ _ _ _ |

# Where in the house?

*You will hear a series of sentences. Decide where the person, animal, or object is most likely to be. Mark the answer.*

| | | | |
|---|---|---|---|
| 1 | a) in viā | b) in tablīnō | c) in triclīniō |
| 2 | a) in culīnā | b) in viā | c) in tablīnō |
| 3 | a) in viā | b) in cubiculō | c) in ātriō |
| 4 | a) in hortō | b) in lātrīnā | c) in impluviō |
| 5 | a) in lātrīnā | b) in viā | c) in impluviō |

## 1.3   What's in a name?

1   *It may surprise you to discover what some Latin names mean. Match the names in the left-hand column with a Latin word and its meaning in the column on the right. Put the appropriate letter next to the name.*

|   |   |   |   |
|---|---|---|---|
| i) | Clēmēns | a) | quīntus (fifth) |
| ii) | Jūlius | b) | Iovilius (descended from Jove) |
| iii) | Caesar | c) | clēmentia (mercy) |
| iv) | Claudius | d) | fēlīcitās (luck) |
| v) | Quīntus | e) | claudus (lame, limping) |
| vi) | Fēlīx | f) | caesariēs (head of hair) |

2   *You know that names have a meaning. Below you will find some names which come to us from the Latin language. Say what you think the name might mean. You may be given a word clue in brackets.*

| | | | |
|---|---|---|---|
| Victor/Victoria | _____ | Rex (regal) | _____ |
| Serena | _____ | Rosa | _____ |
| Flora | _____ | Amanda | _____ |
| Gloria | _____ | Leo | _____ |
| Stella | _____ | Max (maximum) | _____ |
| Carmen | _____ | Miranda | _____ |

3   *Use the library or the Internet to find out the meaning of your name.*

4   *Some of our surnames have meanings which relate to a job or profession or skill, for example Cook. Give three more surnames of this type.*

## 1.4   Word Building

*Each of the following formulae represents a word derived from one of the Vocabulary Checklist words for this Stage. Combine the suffixes (in capital letters) with the Latin root suggested by the English word in lower-case letters to form the derivative. Watch for simple spelling changes in the root.*

1   street + DUCT       3   work + OUS       5   father + MONY
2   slave + TUDE        4   sit + MENT

## 1.5  in vīllā

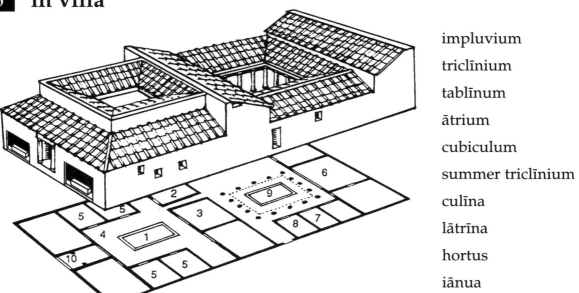

impluvium

triclīnium

tablīnum

ātrium

cubiculum

summer triclīnium

culīna

lātrīna

hortus

iānua

*Fill in the spaces below with the correct English and Latin names, and numbers from the ground plan. Use the clues to help you.*

| English | Clues | Latin | Number |
|---|---|---|---|
| dining room | Three couches here. Clue: *tri*plet, *tri*o, *tri*cycle | _____ | 2 |
| hall | The first big room you enter | _____ | _____ |
| garden | For people interested in *horticulture* | _____ | _____ |
| door | A *janitor* might sit on duty here | _____ | _____ |
| rainwater pool | French clue: *il pleut* | _____ | _____ |
| _____ | Very small room, not used much by day | cubiculum | _____ |
| _____ | A *table* would be necessary here | tablīnum | 3 |
| _____ | Sometimes called *latrine* today | lātrīna | 8 |
| _____ | Near the lātrīna. Grumio's workplace | culīna | _____ |
| summer _____ | A pleasant place to eat in the summer | summer _____ | _____ |

## 1.6 How is Latin pronounced?

*Circle the English word that has the same (or almost the same) sound as the letters in boldface in the Latin words.*

1  Qu**ī**ntus  bit  price  machine
2  C**ae**cilius  high  lay  neat
3  p**a**ter  make  about  far
4  Cl**ēmēns**  answer  enzyme  insurance
5  c**u**līna  fume  put  boot
6  **c**anis  century  cat  chimney
7  Metel**la**  brilliant  immortal life  hall
8  sur**g**it  angel  give  hello
9  **v**ia  waste  violet  yesterday

## 1.7 Audīte / Dīcite

*Cover half the page. Player **A** sees only the **A** side, and **B** sees only the **B** side. **A** first reads the Latin sentence and the question at 1 (for which the answer is provided). Player **B** listens and then answers the question. **B** then asks the question after sentence 1 in the **B** column. After **A** has answered this question, go on to sentence 2. Repeat as before.*

New question words: **quis** – who?   **quid** – what?   **ubi** – where?

| A | B |
|---|---|
| 1  pater est in tablīnō.<br>ubi est pater? (in tablīnō) | 1  pater est in tablīnō.<br>quis est in tablīnō? (pater) |
| 2  canis est in viā.<br>quid est in viā? (canis) | 2  canis est in viā.<br>ubi est canis? (in viā) |
| 3  Metella in ātriō sedet.<br>ubi est māter? (in ātriō) | 3  Metella in ātriō sedet.<br>quis in ātriō sedet? (Metella) |
| 4  coquus in culīnā dormit.<br>quis in culīnā dormit? (coquus) | 4  coquus in culīnā dormit.<br>ubi est coquus? (in culīnā) |
| 5  Clēmēns in hortō labōrat.<br>ubi est Clēmēns? (in hortō) | 5  Clēmēns in hortō labōrat.<br>quis in hortō labōrat? (Clēmēns) |
| 6  fīlius in triclīniō bibit.<br>quis in triclīniō bibit? (fīlius) | 6  fīlius in triclīniō bibit.<br>ubi est fīlius? (in triclīniō) |

## 1.8  Caecilius

*Read pages 10–11 in your textbook and answer the following:*

1  When and where did Caecilius live?

2  What was the population of that town?

3  Where was the town located?

4  Name five of the various jobs Caecilius did.

5  How do we know so much about Caecilius?

6  How did Caecilius obtain his money?

7  What was Caecilius' full name? What does it tell us about him?

8  Name two rights that Caecilius had.

9  What was the one exception to the lack of rights of a slave?

10  Describe the three parts of a Roman name.


## 1.9  Metella

*Read page 12 in your textbook and answer the following:*

1  What were Metella's two main responsibilities?

2  List four of the ways a Roman wife could exercise her influence.

3  List six activities that Roman women could enjoy outside the home.

4  List four of the occupations that some Roman women had.

5  Who was Eumachia? Why was she well known in Pompeii?

## 1.10 Houses in Pompeii

*Read pages 13–15 in your textbook and answer the following:*

1 List three ways a Roman house differed from a modern one.

2 What was the purpose of the house windows?

3 What was often on either side of the front door of a Roman house?

4 What general impression did the exterior give?

5 How many major parts were there to the Roman house?

6 What was the most impressive part of the house? Why was this so?

7 What was the difference between the **compluvium** and **impluvium**?

8 What was the most striking feature of the **ātrium**?

9 Give four details about the furniture and/or decor of the **ātrium**.

10 Describe the doors to the entrances of the rooms arranged around the **ātrium**.

11 List six areas or rooms found in the second part of the typical Roman house.

12 V (**vērum**) or F (**falsum**)?
   a) Roman houses such as Caecilius' were very common.

   b) Shopkeepers often lived over their shops.

   c) Apartment buildings were often several stories high.

13 Identify the following:
   a) triclīnium
   b) tablīnum
   c) larārium
   d) ātrium
   e) cubiculum
   f) culīna
   g) latrīna
   h) hortus
   i) iānua
   j) peristȳlium

# Who does the action? Who or what receives it?

*In each of the Latin sentences below, draw one line under the nominative and two lines under the accusative. Then write a translation for each sentence in the space provided.*

*Translation*

1  Grumiō triclīnium intrat.  _____

2  Grumiō pāvōnem portat.  _____

3  Metella pāvōnem gustat.  _____

4  pāvō Metellam dēlectat.  _____

5  Caecilius quoque pāvōnem gustat.  _____

6  pāvō Caecilium nōn dēlectat.  _____

# Using Latin

*Using your knowledge of Latin, complete the following sentences by circling the correct answer.*

1  A bibulous person likes
  a)  the Bible        b)  drinking        c)  growing bulbs

**Bibulous** comes from the Latin word _____ .

2  A cantata is
  a)  sung        b)  danced        c)  recited

**Cantata** comes from the Latin word _____ .

3  A recumbent person is
  a)  standing to attention    b)  lying down        c)  running

**Recumbent** comes from the Latin word _____ .

4  An impecunious person
  a)  has no money        b)  is unintelligent    c)  is impolite

**Impecunious** comes from the Latin word _____ .

5  The optimum number is
  a)  the highest        b)  the lowest        c)  the best

**Optimum** comes from the Latin word _____ .

## 2.3 Which answers are possible?

1 What does Metella taste? *Circle the things Metella would enjoy tasting.*

canem   culīnam   pecūniam   cēnam   hortum   pāvōnem   coquum

2 Whom does Clemens greet? *Circle only people.*

amīcum   mēnsam   vīllam   mercātōrem   Quīntum   hortum   servum
ancillam   pāvōnem

3 Which rooms does Cerberus enter? *Circle only rooms.*

ātrium   tablīnum   impluvium   cibum   triclīnium   culīnam   lectum
ancillam   vīnum   cubiculum

4 What does Metella do? *Circle actions appropriate for Metella.*

salit   dormit   sedet   clāmat   vīsitat   cēnat   stertit   gustat

5 Whom does Metella hear? *Circle only animals or people.*

fīlium   hortum   mēnsam   canem   coquum   pāvōnem   cēnam
ancillam

6 What does Caecilius do? *Circle actions appropriate for Caecilius.*

scrībit   sedet   pecūniam numerat   lātrat   in lectō recumbit   salit
cantat   coquit


## 2.4 Find the hidden sentence.

1 *In this group, cross out every word describing a **person**.*
*Translate the sentence that remains.*

māter   coquus   canis   fīlius   servus   pater   argentārius
in impluviō   ancilla   dominus   stat

2 *In this group, cross out every word describing **movement**.*
*Translate the sentence that remains.*

salit   pater   surgit   exit   coquum   portat   vīsitat   vituperat   intrat

3 *In this group, cross out every **accusative case**.*
*Translate the sentence that remains.*

cibum   culīnam   canis   amīcum   servum   pāvōnem   ancillam
mercātōrem   est   pecūniam   pestis   iānuam   fīlium

**Cerberus**

1 *Fill in the missing Latin word which matches the English or the picture. You will not use all the items in the lists.*

| Nominative | Accusative | Verbs |
| --- | --- | --- |
| Caecilius | Caecilium | clāmat |
| canis | canem | est |
| cēna | cēnam | exit |
| Cerberus | Cerberum | gustat |
| coquus | coquum | intrat |
| culīna | culīnam | laudat |
| dominus | dominum | parat |
| Grumiō | Grumiōnem | salūtat |
| servus | servum | stat |

_____ est in culīnā. coquus _____

(dinner)

parat. Caecilius culīnam _____ . _____ cibum

(enters)        (The master)

gustat. Caecilius _____ laudat. Cerberus _____ intrat.

(the cook)        (the kitchen)

_____ cibum videt. _____ cibum gustat.

(The dog)

Grumiō _____ videt. _____ nōn est laetus.

(the dog)        (The slave)

"pestis!" _____ clāmat. _____ est īrātus.

(the cook)

"furcifer!" dominus _____ . Cerberus exit.

(shouts)

2 *Now translate the story.*

**13**

**amīcus Grumiōnem vīsitat.**

*Your job is to put the jumbled pictures in the right order. Listen to the story. Every time your teacher stops, number the picture which illustrates what has been read.*

*Now read the longer version of this story in Stage 2. Pick out a suitable Latin sentence for each picture and write this on the lines provided.*

# Roman Dinner Parties

| gustātiō<br>Starters | prīmae mēnsae<br>Main dishes | secundae mēnsae<br>Desserts |
|---|---|---|
| Leeks with olives | Stuffed hare with white sauce, dried peas, and leeks | Dates stuffed with nuts and pine kernels fried in honey |
| Snails fried in oil, garum, and pepper | Fallow deer roasted with onion sauce, Jericho dates, raisins, oil, and honey | Pastry cases filled with honey and walnuts |
| Sows' udders stuffed with salted sea-urchins | Dormice stuffed with pork and pine kernels | Milk and egg sweet |
| Mussels in sweet wine sauce | Ham boiled with figs and baked in pastry with honey | Fresh fruit – pomegranates, apples, grapes, plums |
| Boiled tree fungi with peppered garum sauce | Boiled chicken with dill sauce, cabbage, and green lentils | |
| | Mulsum – wine mixed with honey | |

**Martial invites a friend to dinner.**

You'll have a nice meal, Julius, at my house; do come if you've nothing better to do. Keep the eighth hour (two o'clock) free; we'll go to Stephanus' baths beforehand, just next door. For starters, you'll get lettuce, fresh young leeks, then salted tuna a little bigger than a mackerel and garnished with eggs done up with rue; then more eggs, this time baked to a turn in a moderate oven with cheese and olives. For the main course, you can have fish and oysters, sow-belly, chicken, and duck. I promise I won't recite anything, but you can read me your poem *The Giants* again, or recite some of the ones about the countryside.

**Pliny complains about a guest who failed to turn up.**

What do you mean by accepting my invitation to dinner and then not turning up? It was all set out, a lettuce each, three snails, two eggs, barley-water, wine with honey, chilled with snow (an expensive item, please note, since it disappears in the dish!), some olives, beets, gherkins, onions, and plenty of other delicacies as well. You could have had a comic play, a poetry reading, or a singer. But no, instead you preferred to go where you could have oysters, sows' innards, sea urchins, and Spanish dancing girls!

*Design an invitation to a* **cēna,** *using Roman names and referring to Roman customs. Select your menu and describe the entertainments.*

## 2.8 More about Roman Food

Ordinary Romans did not eat much meat. Their main food was wheat flour, which was made into bread or porridge. They added herbs, vegetables, and other flavorings to make their simple diet more interesting.

Wealthy people had a more varied menu and ate much more meat and fish. A favorite sauce was the strong, salty **garum**, made from fish entrails. At a **cēna** people might eat as many as seven courses.

1   *There is one food in each group which the Romans did **not** eat. Circle it and pick out from the word the letter indicated in the column on the right. Rearrange the letters to complete the sentence below.*

   a) potatoes   cabbage   onions   olives        2nd letter _____

   b) chicken   lamb   curry   mushrooms        5th letter _____

   c) figs   raisins   chocolate   pears          2nd letter _____

   d) cherries   bananas   dates   walnuts        3rd letter _____

   e) tea   wine   olive-oil   fish-sauce          2nd letter _____

   The Romans relied on ___ ___ ___ ___ ___ as a sweetener

2   *Spot the differences. There are five things missing in one of these pictures of a* **cēna***.*

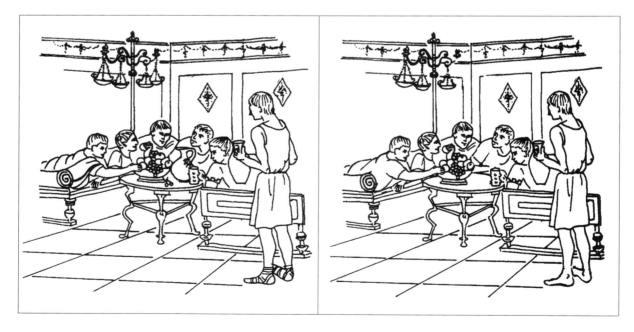

**Audīte / Dīcite**

*Cover half the page. Player **A** sees only the **A** side, and **B** sees only the **B** side. **A** first reads the Latin sentence and the question at 1 (for which the answer is provided). Player **B** listens and then answers the question. **B** then asks the question after sentence 1 in the **B** column. After **A** has answered this question, go on to sentence 2. Repeat as before.*

New question word: **quem** – whom?

| **A** | **B** |
|---|---|
| 1  amīcus in hortō sedet.<br>quis in hortō sedet? (amīcus) | 1  amīcus in hortō sedet.<br>ubi est amīcus? (in hortō) |
| 2  toga est in cubiculō.<br>ubi est toga? (in cubiculō) | 2  toga est in cubiculō.<br>quid est in cubiculō? (toga) |
| 3  fīlius patrem salūtat.<br>quis patrem salūtat? (fīlius) | 3  fīlius patrem salūtat.<br>quem fīlius salūtat? (patrem) |
| 4  Metella Grumiōnem spectat.<br>quem Metella spectat?<br>   (Grumiōnem) | 4  Metella Grumiōnem spectat.<br>quis Grumiōnem spectat?<br>   (Metella) |
| 5  mercātor cēnam gustat.<br>quis cēnam gustat? (mercātor) | 5  mercātor cēnam gustat.<br>quid mercātor gustat? (cēnam) |
| 6  Caecilius cibum laudat.<br>quid Caecilius laudat? (cibum) | 6  Caecilius cibum laudat.<br>quis cibum laudat? (Caecilius) |
| 7  coquus amīcum vituperat.<br>quis amīcum vituperat?<br>   (coquus) | 7  coquus amīcum vituperat.<br>quem coquus vituperat?<br>   (amīcum) |
| 8  Clēmēns vīnum portat.<br>quid Clēmēns portat? (vīnum) | 8  Clēmēns vīnum portat.<br>quis vīnum portat? (Clēmēns) |

## 2.10 Daily Life

*Read pages 30–32 in your textbook and answer the following:*

1  As you read these pages, list, in order, the parts of Caecilius' day.

2  Name the items of clothing that Caecilius would put on.

3  Name the items of clothing Metella would put on.

4  Besides helping her dress, how else would Metella's slaves assist her in the morning?

5  What did the Romans eat for breakfast?

6  Identify the following:
   a) **salūtātiō**      b) **clientēs**      c) **patrōnus**

7  Where did Caecilius probably have his banker's stall?

8  When was lunch? What did the Pompeians usually eat?

9  What was the Latin name for the main meal of the day? When was it served?

10  Write four details about the Roman dining room and/or Roman dining customs.

11  List some of the foods in the Roman dinner.
   a) appetizers
   b) main course
   c) desserts

## 3.1   What is the name?

*Find the name of the region where Pompeii was located. First fill each set of blanks with a Latin adjective which translates the English. Then write the numbered letters in the order of their numbers in the space below.*

angry

                      5
___ ___ ___ ___ ___ ___

satisfied

      1
___ ___ ___ ___ ___ ___ ___ ___

busy

                2
___ ___ ___ ___ ___ ___ ___ ___

terrified

      4
___ ___ ___ ___ ___ ___ ___ ___ ___ ___

much

      3
___ ___ ___ ___ ___ ___

very good

           7
___ ___ ___ ___ ___ ___

happy

      8
___ ___ ___ ___ ___

big

        6
___ ___ ___ ___ ___ ___

       1  2  3  4  5  6  7  8

Name: ___ ___ ___ ___ ___ ___ ___ ___

## 3.2   What kind of person is he or she?

1  quālis coquus est Grumiō?
    What kind of cook is Grumio?

    *Circle adjectives that describe Grumio.*

    laetus

    magnus

    occupātus

    multus

    Graecus

2  quālis ancilla est Melissa?
    What kind of slave-girl is Melissa?

    *Circle adjectives that describe Melissa.*

    pulchra

    occupāta

    docta

    magna

    Graeca

## 3.3 How are these words connected?

*Each of the Latin words in the box is connected with an English word in the list below. Match up the English and Latin words. Then show what their connection is. Use a dictionary to help you if necessary. The first one is done for you.*

| stat | portat | clāmat | dominus |
| vīnum | māter | audit | |

| | English | Latin | Connection |
|---|---|---|---|
| 1 | stationary | stat | standing still |
| 2 | maternal | | |
| 3 | auditorium | | |
| 4 | clamor | | |
| 5 | dominate | | |
| 6 | vinegar | | |
| 7 | porter | | |

## 3.4 vērum aut falsum?

*Your teacher will read four sentences about each picture. Decide whether each statement is* vērum *or* falsum *and write the answers (V or F) underneath the picture.*

 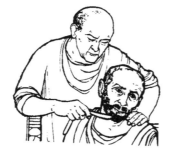 

A 1 __ 2 __ 3 __ 4 __     B 1 __ 2 __ 3 __ 4 __     C 1 __ 2 __ 3 __ 4 __

**Celer, Pantagathus, Syphāx**

*Here are some words taken from the stories in this Stage and pictures of the main characters in the stories. Write beside the pictures the words that are connected with each character and give their meaning.*

| | | | | |
|---|---|---|---|---|
| tondet | vēnālīcius | leō | nāvis | pictūra |
| secat | triclīnium | pingit | taberna | servus |
| emit | tōnsor | novācula | pictor | ancilla |

Celer

Latin word · Meaning

1 _____ _____
2 _____ _____
3 _____ _____
4 _____ _____
5 _____ _____

Pantagathus

Latin word · Meaning

1 _____ _____
2 _____ _____
3 _____ _____
4 _____ _____
5 _____ _____

Syphāx

Latin word · Meaning

1 _____ _____
2 _____ _____
3 _____ _____
4 _____ _____
5 _____ _____

**21**

**Who's who?**

*Read each sentence. Then replace the name in boldface with a word which shows the person's job or position. Use the words in the box below, making sure you have chosen the correct case. By the end you should have used each word once.*

| | | | |
|---|---|---|---|
| ancilla | ancillam | māter | mātrem |
| pictor | pictōrem | argentārius | argentārium |
| coquus | coquum | servus | servum |
| tōnsor | tōnsōrem | vēnālīcius | vēnālīcium |

For example: **Clēmēns** vīnum portat.     vēnālīcius **Melissam** laudat.
**servus** vīnum portat.     vēnālīcius **ancillam** laudat.

1 **Caecilius** pecūniam numerat.

_____ pecūniam numerat.

2 amīcus **Caecilium** salūtat.

amīcus _____ salūtat.

3 **Clēmēns** ātrium intrat.

_____ ātrium intrat.

4 **Metella** cibum gustat.

_____ cibum gustat.

5 dominus **Melissam** emit.

dominus _____ emit.

6 **Celer** iānuam pulsat.

_____ iānuam pulsat.

7 fīlius **Clēmentem** vocat.

fīlius _____ vocat.

8 dominus **Grumiōnem** laudat.

dominus _____ laudat.

9 **Pantagathus** barbam tondet.

_____ barbam tondet.

10 **Grumiō** cēnam coquit.

_____ cēnam coquit.

11 mercātor **Syphācem** quaerit.

mercātor _____ quaerit.

12 canis **Celerem** audit.

canis _____ audit.

13 **Melissa** linguam Latīnam discit.

_____ linguam Latīnam discit.

14 canis **Metellam** spectat.

canis _____ spectat.

15 senex **Pantagathum** vituperat.

senex _____ vituperat.

16 **Syphāx** servum habet.

_____ servum habet.

# In Pompeii

*Match each of the letters on the plan of Pompeii with one of the clues given below.*

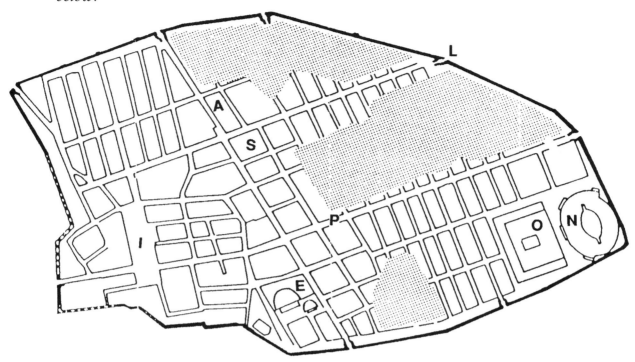

If you want to see a play,
Hurry here without delay.

Here you come to buy and sell,
To vote, to pray, to chat as well.

Eight of these about the town:
Some lead up, and some lead down!

See the different painted signs
Advertising food and wines.

Watch the gladiators fight!
A bloody but exciting sight.

Here are games of every sort;
Throw, jump, or wrestle – choose
    your sport!

Four sets around to keep you clean:
Rooms cool or hot, or in between.

This is where our banker is
When not at work – this
    house is his!

*Now rearrange the letters to form the name of a nearby town northwest of Pompeii.*

*By what name is it now known?*

**Audīte / Dīcite**

*Cover half the page. Player **A** sees only the **A** side, and **B** sees only the **B** side.
**A** first reads the Latin sentence and the question at 1 (for which the answer is
provided). Player **B** listens and then answers the question. **B** then asks the
question after sentence 1 in the **B** column. After **A** has answered this question,
go on to sentence 2. Repeat as before.*

New question word: **quālis** – what kind of?

| **A** | **B** |
|---|---|
| 1 amīcus leōnem videt.<br>quis leōnem videt? (amīcus) | 1 amīcus leōnem videt.<br>quid amīcus videt? (leōnem) |
| 2 magnus leō surgit.<br>quālis leō surgit? (magnus) | 2 magnus leō surgit.<br>quid surgit? (leō) |
| 3 Celer pictūram pulchram pingit.<br>quid Celer pingit? (pictūram) | 3 Celer pictūram pulchram pingit.<br>quālem pictūram Celer pingit? (pulchram) |
| 4 Caecilius pictōrem laudat.<br>quem Caecilius laudat? (pictōrem) | 4 Caecilius pictōrem laudat.<br>quis pictōrem laudat? (Caecilius) |
| 5 mercātor forum circumspectat.<br>quis forum circumspectat? (mercātor) | 5 mercātor forum circumspectat.<br>quid mercātor circumspectat? (forum) |
| 6 senex in tabernā sedet.<br>ubi est senex? (in tabernā) | 6 senex in tabernā sedet.<br>quis in tabernā sedet? (senex) |
| 7 tōnsor barbam tondet.<br>quid tōnsor tondet? (barbam) | 7 tōnsor barbam tondet.<br>quis barbam tondet? (tōnsor) |
| 8 poēta versum recitat.<br>quis versum recitat? (poēta) | 8 poēta versum recitat.<br>quid poēta recitat? (versum) |

## 3.9 The Town of Pompeii

*Read pages 43–47 in your textbook and answer the following:*

1 What was Pompeii built upon? How far away was it from Mt. Vesuvius?

2 What types of people were attracted to this Campanian area?

3 Give two reasons why they were attracted to this area.

4 How large was Pompeii? What protected the town?

5 Give the modern names for the two wide main streets of Pompeii.

6 Give four details describing Pompeian streets.

7 What were the two main shopping areas in the city?

8 How were different types of stores indicated?

9 Describe how advertisements and public notices were handled.

10 The forum was the center for many aspects of Pompeian life. Give three of them.

11 Write down one thing you learned about each of the following:
   a) large theater    b) small theater    c) amphitheater

12 List six nationalities you might have met in Pompeii.

13 From where did Pompeii get its water? How was the water stored?

14 Explain the different ways in which people obtained water.

15 How did Rome ensure peace and stable government?

16 Give the two methods of travel and transport used throughout the Empire.

## 4.1  What are you doing?

*Circle the correct verb when a choice is provided in parentheses.*

1 Caecilius says, "Celer is painting."
  Caecilius asks,
    "quid tū (pingō/pingis)?"
  Celer answers,
    "ego leōnem (pingō/pingis)."

2 Metella says, "Clemens is carrying
    something."
  Metella asks,
    "quid tū (portās/portō)?"
  Clemens answers,
    "ego vīnum (portās/portō)."

3 Caecilius says, "The old man
    sees something."
  Caecilius asks,
    "quid tū (vidēs/videō)?"
  The old man answers,
    "ego novāculam
    (vidēs/videō)."

4 The poet says, "Hermogenes has
    something."
  The poet asks,
    "quid tū (habeō/habēs)?"
  Hermogenes answers,
    "ego pecūniam (habeō/habēs)."

5 Quintus says, "Syphax is
    selling someone."
  Quintus asks, "quem tū
    (vēndō/vēndis)?"
  Syphax answers,
    "ego servum
    (vēndō/vēndis)."

## 4.2  Find the verbs.

*In the box of letters below, you will find fourteen verbs with the ending T (e.g. INQUIT). Find each verb and circle it.*

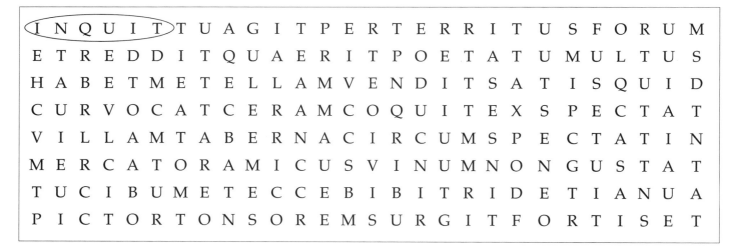

```
I N Q U I T T U A G I T P E R T E R R I T U S F O R U M
E T R E D D I T Q U A E R I T P O E T A T U M U L T U S
H A B E T M E T E L L A M V E N D I T S A T I S Q U I D
C U R V O C A T C E R A M C O Q U I T E X S P E C T A T
V I L L A M T A B E R N A C I R C U M S P E C T A T I N
M E R C A T O R A M I C U S V I N U M N O N G U S T A T
T U C I B U M E T E C C E B I B I T R I D E T I A N U A
P I C T O R T O N S O R E M S U R G I T F O R T I S E T
```

26

**Who am I?**

*On the left you will see a series of sentences followed by the question "quis sum ego?" Write down the answer on the right. The first one is done for you.*

1  ego servum vēndō.
   quis sum ego?                    tū es vēnālīcius!
2  ego pecūniam habeō.
   quis sum ego?                    _____
3  ego barbam tondeō.
   quis sum ego?                    _____
4  ego cibum gustō.
   quis sum ego?                    _____
5  ego in viā dormiō.
   quis sum ego?                    _____
6  ego cēnam coquō.
   quis sum ego?                    _____
7  ego leōnem pingō.
   quis sum ego?                    _____
8  ego in triclīniō bibō.
   quis sum ego?                    _____
9  ego in hortō labōrō.
   quis sum ego?                    _____
10 ego linguam Latīnam discō.
   quis sum ego?                    _____

*Now make up some more examples of your own.*

ego _____
quis sum ego?                    tū _____

ego _____
quis sum ego?                    tū _____

ego _____
quis sum ego?                    tū _____

## 4.4 Links with Latin

*Some European modern languages have words derived from Latin which look so much like the Latin that you can understand them. Match Latin words in the list below with their French, Italian, and Spanish versions and write them in the box; then put the English meaning in the other box. You will not use all the Latin words in the list.*

| | | | | |
|---|---|---|---|---|
| ego respondeō | ego accūsō | ego dēbeō | ego portō | ego vēndō |
| tū respondēs | tū accūsās | tū dēbēs | tū portās | tū vēndis |

**French, Italian, Spanish**       **Latin**       **English**

French: j'accuse

Italian: io accuso

Spanish: yo acuso

---

French: tu vends

Italian: tu vendi

Spanish: tu vendes

---

French: tu réponds

Italian: tu rispondi

---

Italian: io devo

Spanish: yo debo

---

French: je porte

Italian: io porto

28

## 4.5 forum aut basilica?

*In this Stage you have learned about the business that was done in the forum and you have seen a trial in the basilica. Here are some words connected with either the forum or the basilica. Put them into their correct column below.*

| | | | | |
|---|---|---|---|---|
| taberna | testis | emit | tōnsor | rem nōn probat |
| iūdex | vēndit | accūsat | convincit | argentāria |

**forum**                                      **basilica**

1 _____            1 _____

2 _____            2 _____

3 _____            3 _____

4 _____            4 _____

5 _____            5 _____

## 4.6 Word Study

**A** *Circle the word which does not come from the same root as the others.*

1 ambiguous   actor   retroactive   prohibit

2 acquisitive   quibble   inquiry   unquestionably

3 signify   assignment   seal   satisfaction

4 behave   able   cohabit   inhibit

5 jungle   adjudicate   misjudge   injudicious

**B** *Fill in the word or phrase from the list below to complete each sentence.*

assets   habeas corpus   inquest   irrevocable   quorum

1 An _____ will investigate the fatal accident.

2 What is required for a _____? If there are not enough members, we will not be able to conduct business.

3 A writ of _____ will require the defendant to appear.

4 If he refuses, contact the bank and seize his _____.

5 You may want to pause a moment before you make such an _____ decision.

# Finding Your Way around the Forum

*Match the letters in the picture with the clues below.*

1   This is a good place to stroll in the heat of the day.   _____

2   Walk this way for the meeting hall of the clothworkers.   _____

3   Upright stones stop wheeled traffic from entering.   _____

4   It is easier to see and hear political speakers from here.   _____

5   The ash from this will cover the **forum** completely.   _____

6   Head this way for the **basilica**.   _____

7   This famous citizen in the **forum** is not alive.   _____

8   The latest election result can be read from these boards.   _____

9   The Temple of Jupiter stands at the north end.   _____

10   Their togas tell you they are Roman citizens.   _____

11   **amphorae** are large clay jars for storing wine or oil.   _____

12   No carriages allowed? It doesn't matter if you can afford to be carried in a **lectīca**.   _____

Now work out the rest of this sentence.

        (1) (4)    (6) (2) (3) (8) (10)    (7) (5) (9) (12)(11)

Caecilius __ __   __ __ __ __ __   __ __ __ __ __

**30**

## 4.8 The Forum

*Read pages 62–66 in your textbook and answer the following:*

1 What were the three major purposes of the forum in Pompeii?

2 What were its dimensions? What kind of floor did it have?

3 Whose statues stood there?

4 What two protections did the surrounding colonnade provide?

5 How did people enter the forum?

6 What was the purpose of the large stone blocks at the entrance ways?

7 Explain how important information was disseminated among the people.

8 What do these terms mean?
   a) aedile
   b) tribunal
   c) **duovirī**

9 List the five religious shrines around or near the forum.

10 Name the foreign goddess whose temple was in Pompeii.

11 List three things of concern to Apollo.
   List two things of concern to Venus.

12 Why was Venus important to the people of Pompeii?

13 Name two types of markets which existed in the town.

14 Why was the meeting hall of the clothworkers so large?

15 List the possible purposes for the four municipal buildings.

16 What were two major functions of the basilica?

## 5.1 | Compliments or Insults?

*Would you be pleased if someone used the following words to describe you?*
*Answer yes or no; give the meaning of the word and the Latin word from which*
*it comes. Use an English dictionary to help you if necessary.*

|  | Y/N | Meaning | Latin word |
|---|---|---|---|
| 1 magnificent | ____ | _____ | _____ |
| 2 ridiculous | ____ | _____ | _____ |
| 3 servile | ____ | _____ | _____ |
| 4 mendacious | ____ | _____ | _____ |
| 5 responsive | ____ | _____ | _____ |
| 6 judicious | ____ | _____ | _____ |
| 7 egotistical | ____ | _____ | _____ |
| 8 circumspect | ____ | _____ | _____ |
| 9 tenacious | ____ | _____ | _____ |
| 10 scurrilous | ____ | _____ | _____ |
| 11 pulchritudinous | ____ | _____ | _____ |
| 12 insignificant | ____ | _____ | _____ |
| 13 pestiferous | ____ | _____ | _____ |
| 14 mercenary | ____ | _____ | _____ |

*What do you notice about the endings of seven of the English words on the left?*

*Think of three other examples of describing words (adjectives) with the same*
*ending.*

**Singular or Plural?**

*Your teacher will read eight sentences in Latin. Each of them describes one of the pictures below. As you hear each sentence, write the picture letter in the box next to the sentence number.*

A

B

C

D

E

F

G

H

1 ☐  3 ☐  5 ☐  7 ☐

2 ☐  4 ☐  6 ☐  8 ☐

## 5.3 Latin Words in English

*Latin words that are used in English often form their plural in the Latin way.*
*Fill in the blanks below.*

| Singular | Plural |
| --- | --- |
| cactus | _____ |
| _____ | formulae |
| _____ | narcissi |
| axis | _____ |
| _____ | radii |
| larva | _____ |
| fungus | _____ |
| _____ | appendices |
| vertebra | _____ |
| matrix | _____ |

The crocodiles call us hippopotamuses; we think _____ is more elegant.

## 5.4 Find the hidden sentence.

1   *In this group of words cross out every **plural** word. Translate the sentence that remains.*
    mercātōrēs   āctōrēs   nūntius   fēminae   servī
    agricolae   in forō   nautae   pāstōrēs   clāmat

2   *In this group cross out every word relating to the **theater**. Translate the sentence that remains.*
    āctor   scaena   Pompēiānī   plaudunt   ad urbem
    spectat   fābula   theātrum   contendunt   spectātor

3   *In this group cross out every **plural** word. Translate the sentence that remains.*
    petunt   labōrant   senex   spectant   ambulant
    in theātrō   plaudunt   stant   dormit   sedent

4   *In this group cross out every word relating to **sound**. Translate the sentence that remains.*
    audit   servus   clāmor   in vīllā   plaudit
    cantant   lātrat   vocant   manet   recitat

34

1  *Write each letter from the plan in its correct box.*

[ ]  Pompēiānī theātrum intrant.

[ ]  āctōrēs fābulam agunt.

[ ]  spectātōrēs fābulam exspectant.

2  *Mark the correct answer to complete the sentence.*

Town councilors had seats:
a) at the back
b) at the front

Seats were made of:
a) wood
b) stone

The cost of admission:
a) varied
b) was free

The performances lasted:
a) all day
b) until noon

Between plays attendants:
a) made offerings to the gods
b) sprinkled scented water

The large theater was provided with:
a) a roof
b) a canvas awning

The **cavea** was:
a) the back wall of the stage
b) the seating area

Expenses were paid by:
a) the town council
b) a wealthy citizen

Plays were put on:
a) several times a year
b) every market day

On the day of a performance:
a) shops were closed
b) business increased

3  *Underline the word which would NOT apply to the spectators.*

| SEDENT | PLAUDUNT | SPECTANT |
|---|---|---|
| 14  11  15 | 13  12 | 8  9  3 |

| LABORANT | CLAMANT | AUDIUNT |
|---|---|---|
| 4  5  7 | 2  16  10 | 1  6  17 |

*Rearrange the letters in the order indicated above to form a Latin sentence. Put X on the plan above where this would happen and translate the sentence.*

_ _ _ _ _ _   _ _   _ _ _ _ _ _   _ _ _

**Audīte / Dīcite**

A *and* B *alternate reading the sentences aloud (selecting the correct choice from parentheses) and translating them into English.* A *reads and translates the odd sentences, with verification from* B. B *reads and translates the even sentences, with verification from* A.

**A**

1 (mercātor/mercātōrēs) forum intrant.

2 dominus servum vocat.
The master calls the slave.

3 (canis/canēs) in viā sedet.

4 pater in basilicā labōrat.
Father is working in the basilica.

5 (fēmina/fēminae) stolam emit.

6 puellae nōn adsunt.
The girls are not here.

7 (amīcus/amīcī) vīnum exspectat.

8 senēs ad triclīnium contendunt.
The old men hurry to the dining room.

9 (puer/puerī) sunt in hortō.

10 iuvenis clāmōrem audit.
The young man hears the uproar.

11 (agricola/agricolae) ad urbem currunt.

12 āctōrēs in theātrō stant.
The actors are standing in the theater.

**B**

1 mercātōrēs forum intrant.
The merchants enter the forum.

2 (dominus/dominī) servum vocat.

3 canis in viā sedet.
The dog is sitting in the street.

4 (pater/patrēs) in basilicā labōrat.

5 fēmina stolam emit.
The woman is buying a dress.

6 (puella/puellae) nōn adsunt.

7 amīcus vīnum exspectat.
The friend is waiting for the wine.

8 (senex/senēs) ad triclīnium contendunt.

9 puerī sunt in hortō.
The boys are in the garden.

10 (iuvenis/iuvenēs) clāmōrem audit.

11 agricolae ad urbem currunt.
The farmers are running to the city.

12 (āctor/āctōrēs) in theātrō stant.

# 5.7  The Theater at Pompeii

*Read pages 81–84 in your textbook and answer the following:*

1  When were plays performed in Pompeii?

2  What three types of people went to plays?

3  What three things might they take with them to the theater?

4  Who did not have to hurry to the plays? Why not?

5  Where were latecomers seated?

6  How many people could the large open-air theater hold?

7  What was the Odeon?

8  Identify:
   a) the **cavea**
   b) the **orchēstra**
   c) the **scaena**
   d) the **scaenae frōns**

9  What was the admission charge to the theater?

10  Who paid the theatrical production expenses? For what two reasons did he do this?

11  List three possible sources of relief from the heat of the sun.

12  What was the pantomime?

13  What performers did it require?

14  Who were the actors of the community?

15  What were farces?

16  When were they usually performed?

17  How did the audience recognize the characters?

18  What were these things made of?

19  Name two famous writers of Roman comedies.

## 6.1  What is the Latin message?

*First fill each set of blanks with the letters of an English word which is related to the Latin one in parentheses. Use the English definition to help you find the English word that fits the blanks. Then write the numbered letters in the order of their numbers in the spaces provided.*

First word of message:

|  |  |  |
|---|---|---|
| (currit) | flow, as of electricity | _ _ _ _ _ _<br>          4 |
| (cubiculum) | small space or compartment | _ _ _ _ _ _<br>  2 |
| (dormit) | inactive | _ _ _ _ _ _<br>      6 |
| (ambulat) | vehicle for carrying sick | _ _ _ _ _ _ _<br>  1 |
| (fābula) | story with a moral | _ _ _ _ _<br>      3 |
| (coquit) | bread in small, rough cake | _ _ _ _ _ _<br>        5 |

1  2  3  4  5  6

Hidden Latin word (1): _ _ _ _ _ _

Second word of message:

|  |  |  |
|---|---|---|
| (scrībit) | sacred book | _ _ _ _ _ _ _ _<br>  4 |
| (fortis) | a large fort | _ _ _ _ _ _ _<br>          6 |
| (clāmat) | assert as a fact | _ _ _ _ _<br>      2 |
| (signum) | make known by signs | _ _ _ _ _ _<br>  5 |
| (vēndit) | person who sells things | _ _ _ _ _ _<br>      1 |
| (manet) | large or stately residence | _ _ _ _ _ _<br>  3 |

1  2  3  4  5  6

Hidden Latin word (2): _ _ _ _ _ _

*Read and translate the hidden message.*

**38**

## 6.2 Pure Form-alities

1  *Circle the correct noun form in each sentence. Translate into English.*
   a) (māter/mātrem) īnfantem tenēbat.
   b) īnfāns (mātrem/māter) spectābat.
   c) (amīcus/amīcum) poētam audīvit.
   d) poēta (amīcus/amīcum) vituperāvit.

2  *Circle the correct verb form in each sentence. Translate into English.*
   a) argentārius in forō (labōrābat/labōrābant).
   b) mercātōrēs ad argentāriam (festīnāvit/festīnāvērunt).
   c) amīcī pecūniam (quaerēbat/quaerēbant).
   d) sed agricola argentārium (vituperābat/vituperābant).

3  *Circle the correct verb form in each set of parentheses. Translate into English.*
   a) tū amīcum ad vīllam (invītās/invītat); ego (sum/es) sōlus.
   b) tū cēnam optimam (parat/parās); ego nihil (cōnsūmit/cōnsūmō).
   c) amīcus vīllam (intrat/intrās); ego in viā (manēs/maneō).
   d) tū (es/est) laetus; ego (lacrimō/lacrimās).

## 6.3 pugna

*You have met the following words which have some connection with fighting. Choose **SIX** of them and give an English derivative for each. Show that you know what the English word means by including it in a sentence of your own. Use a dictionary to help you if necessary.*

| pugna fortis superāvit clāmor pulsāvit īrātus incitābant vexābat |
| --- |

# After or Because?

*Complete each sentence with the most suitable group of words below.*

postquam fābulam spectāvērunt     quod cēna erat optima
quod dominus dormiēbat     postquam ānulum spectāvit
postquam tabernam intrāvit     quod erant īrātī

1   amīcī, _____, coquum laudābant.

2   agricolae, _____, mercātōrem pulsābant.

3   iūdex, _____, Hermogenem vituperāvit.

4   Pompēiānī, _____, āctōrēs laudāvērunt.

5   Caecilius, _____, vīnum gustāvit.

6   servus, _____, nōn labōrābat.

# What did they do?

*Your teacher will read a sentence to you with the last word left out. Underline the verb which would complete the sentence. The first four have pictures.*

1
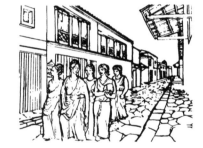
numerāvit / numerāvērunt

2

ambulābat / ambulābant

3

sedēbat / sedēbant

4

vēndēbat / vēndēbant

5   recitāvit / recitāvērunt     6   pulsāvit / pulsāvērunt
7   labōrābat / labōrābant     8   festīnāvit / festīnāvērunt

## 6.6 poēta et canis

*Translate the story into English.*

1  Fēlīx et amīcī in tabernā bibēbant.
   poēta intrāvit.

2  amīcī poētam spectābant; poēta
   cantābat. amīcī nōn erant contentī.
   "satis! satis!" clāmāvērunt.

3  subitō Fēlīx ē tabernā festīnāvit.
   lībertus canem quaesīvit.

4  Fēlīx canem in tabernam portāvit,
   ubi poēta cantābat.

5  canis poētam audīvit, et ferōciter lātrāvit.

6  omnēs amīcī rīdēbant; paene lacrimābant.
   poēta īrātus ē tabernā festīnāvit.

7  Fēlīx et amīcī canem laudāvērunt.
   canis erat laetissimus.

## 6.7   Slaves and Freedmen

*Read pages 97–100 in your textbook and answer the following:*

1   What were two limitations faced by slaves in the Roman world?

2   How did the Romans regard slavery?

3   How were color and slavery connected in Roman times?

4   Describe how the slaves' lives were intertwined with the lives of free people.

5   What were three ways to become a slave?

6   By the first century A.D. what percentage of the Italian population were slaves?

7   How many slaves might very wealthy men own?

8   How many slaves did Caecilius own?

9   What was special about Pedanius Secundus?

10   What was one job carried out by publicly owned slaves in towns?

11   What were four areas where publicly owned slaves worked in the country?

12   What were the strongest slaves used for?

13   What were eight "occupations" of slaves in towns?

14   Why were foreign travelers surprised when they visited Rome or Italy?

15   What usually dictated the way masters treated their slaves?

16   What were **vernae**?

17   What were **alumnī**?

18   What were three ways in which slaves might interact with household children?

19   What were four circumstances under which a slave might be freed?

20   What was the earliest age at which a slave could be freed?

21   What was **manūmissiō**?

22   Describe three ceremonies for freeing slaves.

23   In what two activities could a **lībertus** not participate?

24   In what two activities was a **lībertus** attached to his former master?

25 For what two purposes was a **liberta** often freed?

26 What did a **libertus** take from his master?

27 How could **liberti** earn a living?

28 Who were the Vettii and what of theirs have archaeologists discovered?

29 How was a freedman related to our family in Pompeii?

## 6.8 Word Equations

*Each of the following formulae represents a derivative from the Vocabulary Checklist. Combine the prefixes and/or suffixes (in capital letters) with the Latin root suggested by the English word in lower-case letters to form the derivative. Watch for simple spelling changes in the root. Then find its meaning in the list below and write the number for that meaning in the space ahead of the formula.*

_____ DE + good + AIR = _____

_____ PR + buy + IUM = _____

_____ brave + FY = _____

_____ IM + through + FECT = _____

_____ TRAN + write = _____

1 strengthen
2 copy
3 prize
4 suave
5 faulty

## 7.1   What do you see in the picture?

*First study the picture and then circle the names of all the objects and persons that are pictured, either whole or in part.*

| | |
|---|---|
| amīcus | leō |
| Caecilius | turba |
| cibus | mēnsa |
| cubiculum | pōculum |
| hortus | cēna |
| lectus | triclīnium |
| barba | canis |

## 7.2   fābula mīrābilis

*Look at the picture. Your teacher will read five sentences about it. As you hear each sentence, write its letter in the correct box.*

**The Wasp**

*Translate the sentences below into English.*

1   dominus vespam audīvit. vespam timēbat.

2   dominus servum cōnspexit. servum vocāvit.

3   servus vespam agitābat.  vespam pulsāvit.

4   vespa īrāta erat. servum vulnerāvit.

5   servus clāmābat. vespam vituperāvit.

6   ancilla clāmōrem audīvit.
    vespam necāvit et servum servāvit.

vespam   *a wasp*        vulnerāvit   *wounded*

**Night Horror**

*In the story below, there are many words which come almost directly from Latin. Pick out these words and write them beside the Latin ones below.*

In an agricultural area of Italy, it was a cold, dark night and the moon was obscured by clouds. All the nocturnal animals were awake and made such a noise that they were driving the local inhabitants insane. Suddenly there came a terrifying howl, which filled everyone with horror. One solitary man was brave enough to venture out cautiously into the now deserted outskirts of the village. He feared that he might be in mortal danger, but knew his quest was vital. As the bushes rustled, his pulse beat even faster. Would a terrible apparition rise up in front of him? He felt something brush against his leg – only to realize that the source of his terror was nothing more horrible than a black cat on the prowl.

| Latin word | Word in the story | Latin word | Word in the story |
|------------|-------------------|------------|-------------------|
| appāret | _____ | obscūrus | _____ |
| terret | _____ | vīta | _____ |
| cautē | _____ | agricola | _____ |
| mortuus | _____ | nox, noctem | _____ |
| sōlus | _____ | horribilis | _____ |
| dēsertus | _____ | habitat | _____ |
| pulsat | _____ | īnsānus | _____ |

**Find the roots.**

*Circle the word which does not come from the same root as the others.*

1  lacrimal   lacerate   lachrymose   lacrimation

2  annihilate   nihilism   nibble   nil   annihilation

3  parachute   rampart   partial   separate

4  deter   intern   terrorism   terrific

5  adumbrate   umbrage   somber   ember

**Present or Past?**

*In each Latin sentence, circle the word in the parentheses which correctly translates the English word or words in boldface. Then mark the box which indicates whether the sentence is in present or past time.*

|  | Present | Past |
|---|---|---|

1   Grumio **is preparing** the dinner.
    Grumiō cēnam (parāvit / parat).

2   The spectators **departed**.
    spectātōrēs (discessērunt / discēdunt).

3   The thief **heads for** the bedroom.
    fūr cubiculum (petit / petīvit).

4   Melissa **praised** the actor.
    Melissa āctōrem (laudat / laudāvit).

5   The dogs **frightened** the boy.
    canēs puerum (terruērunt / terrent).

6   The old men **heard** the racket.
    senēs clāmōrem (audīvērunt / audiunt).

7   The slaves **caught sight of** Decens.
    servī Decentem (cōnspiciunt / cōnspexērunt).

8   Grumio and Clemens **found fault with** Melissa.
    Grumiō et Clēmēns Melissam (vituperant / vituperāvērunt).

9   The guests **said**, "Goodbye."
    hospitēs "valē" (dīxērunt / dīcunt).

10  The poet **is walking** in the garden.
    poēta in hortō (ambulat / ambulāvit).

**Food for Ghosts**

*Find the English names of two items which were left beside tombs for the ghosts of the dead.*

*First, fill in each set of blanks with the English which correctly translates the Latin. Then write the numbered letters in the order of their numbers in the spaces provided.*

**One offering of food:**

cēnāvit = he __ __ __ __ __
                4

īnfāns = the __ __ __ __
               1

lacrimat = he __ __ __ __ __
                        5

cōnspicit = he __ __ __ __ __ __ __ __ __ __ __
                   3

intellēxit = he __ __ __ __ __ __ __ __ __ __
                        2

  1  2  3  4  5

Answer: __ __ __ __ __

**Another offering:**

nihil = __ __ __ __ __ __ __
           3

necāvit = he __ __ __ __ __ __
                  2

parat = he __ __ __ __ __ __ __ __
                4

tamen = __ __ __ __ __ __ __
              1

        1  2  3  4

Answer: __ __ __ __

48

**vērum aut falsum: Dead or Alive?**

*Study this picture of Roman tombs. Put V (vērum) or F (falsum) by the statements below.*

1   Look at A. Some tombs looked like small houses.                              ____
2   Look at B. Tombs like this one would belong to someone
    very poor.                                                                   ____
3   Look at C. These tombs lined a road running through the
    center of town.                                                             ____
4   Look at D. Sometimes tombs and monuments like this were
    inscribed with messages or greetings to anyone who passed by. ____
5   Some Romans believed that the dead liked to have their
    possessions with them in the tomb.                                          ____
6   Some families used to hold banquets each year at the tomb
    to remember the dead relative.                                              ____
7   All Romans took the stories about the underworld very
    seriously.                                                                  ____
8   Some Romans agreed with Epicurus that you should enjoy
    this life fully because there was no afterlife.                             ____

This Pompeian tombstone gives advice to any human being (Latin **homō** means human, man). You now know enough Latin to work it out. Fill in the English version beside it.

| | |
|---|---|
| DUM VIVES, HOMO, BIBE | WHILE ____ ____, MAN, ____ |
| NAM POST MORTEM NIHIL EST | FOR ____ ____ THERE ____ ____ |

**Audīte / Dīcite**

*A and B alternate reading the sentences aloud. If the verb is in the present tense, say "hodiē." If the verb is perfect or imperfect, say "heri." A reads the odd sentences with verification from B. B reads the even sentences with verification from A.*

| **A** | **B** |
|---|---|
| 1  amīcī in hortō sedent. | 1  amīcī in hortō sedent. (hodiē) |
| 2  omnēs spectātōrēs valdē plausērunt. (heri) | 2  omnēs spectātōrēs valdē plausērunt. |
| 3  senex multam pecūniam nōn habuit. | 3  senex multam pecūniam nōn habuit. (heri) |
| 4  ingēns turba ad theātrum prōcessit. (heri) | 4  ingēns turba ad theātrum prōcessit. |
| 5  canēs leōnem nōn petunt. | 5  canēs leōnem nōn petunt. (hodiē) |
| 6  turba in viā magnum clāmōrem fēcit. (heri) | 6  turba in viā magnum clāmōrem fēcit. |
| 7  īnfāns in cubiculō dormiēbat. | 7  īnfāns in cubiculō dormiēbat. (heri) |
| 8  fūr tacitē intrāvit quod canēs aderant. (heri) | 8  fūr tacitē intrāvit quod canēs aderant. |
| 9  centuriō nihil audit. | 9  centuriō nihil audit. (hodiē) |
| 10  ancilla lacrimābat quod umbram vīdit. (heri) | 10  ancilla lacrimābat quod umbram vīdit. |
| 11  dominus surgit quod amīcī intrant. | 11  dominus surgit quod amīcī intrant. (hodiē) |
| 12  Clēmēns hospitem quaesīvit. (heri) | 12  Clēmēns hospitem quaesīvit. |

## 7.10 Roman Beliefs about Life after Death

*Read pages 115–118 in your textbook and answer the following:*

1. Where did the Romans bury their dead?

2. Why did they do this (first and third paragraphs, page 115)?

3. Where are the tombs at Pompeii?

4. Briefly describe such tombs:
   a) from the outside
   b) inside.

5. What was the most important thing to provide for the dead person? Why?

6. What did people believe about the "activities" of the dead?

7. Because of this belief, the living provided the dead with two different kinds of things. List more than one example in each category.

8. What did the Romans think ghosts might do if they were not buried properly?

9. Why were holes put in some tombs?

10. Read page 117 and then list four things that Romans might do to make the existence of the dead more cheerful.

11. Identify the following terms from pages 118 and 120:
    a) the Elysian Fields      e) Tartarus
    b) Tityus                  f) Danaus
    c) Sisyphus                g) Ixion
    d) Tantalus

12. To what extent did most Romans in the first century A.D. believe these stories from the Greek myths?

13. Where would they continue to find these stories?

14. Who was Epicurus and what did he teach?

15. What effect would his teaching have on his followers?

16. Why would the majority of Romans not have agreed with these ideas?

## 7.11 Find the verbs.

*In the box of letters below, you will find fifteen verbs with the ending -**NT** (e.g. ABSU**NT**). The tense will be present, imperfect, or perfect. Find each verb and circle it.*

```
A B S U N T A G I T A G U N T E M I S E R U N T
B I B I T E T T U T A N D E M B I B U N T T U M
C U R R E B A N T B I B E R U N T E S T T U U S
N O N T A C I T E D O R M I V E R U N T E X I T
E X S P E C T A N T T E R R E B A N T T A M E N
T E R R E N T E T P R O C E S S E R U N T E S T
P L A U S I T C O N T E N D E R U N T T U R B A
C O N T E N D E B A N T E S T T U M V O C A N T
E X N O N T U R B A V E N E R U N T T E R R A M
```

# Which is the correct accusative?

*First study each picture and then circle the word(s)*
*in parentheses which correctly describe(s) it.*

1  amīcus (canem / canēs ) cōnspexit.

2  Caecilius (cīvem Pompēiānum /
   cīvēs Pompēiānōs) spectābat.

3  Pompēiānī (nūntiōs / nūntium)
   audiēbant.

4  spectātōrēs (murmillōnem /
   murmillōnēs) incitābant.

5  bēstiāriī (bēstiās / bēstiam) necābant.

6  bēstiārius (leōnem / leōnēs) necāvit.

**The Amphitheater**

1   *Look at the plans below. One shows a theater, the other an amphitheater.*

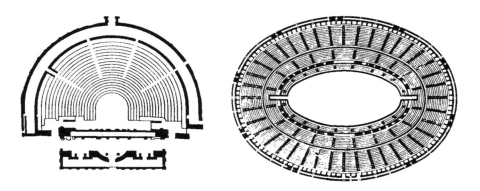

*What do you think the prefix **amphi** means in **amphi**theater?*
***ambi** is another form of the same prefix. What is **amphi** or **ambi***
*about the following?*

a)  an ***amphibious*** animal      _____

b)  an ***ambiguous*** message      _____

c)  an ***ambidextrous*** student   _____

2   *Below you will see a list of Latin words connected with the amphitheater.*
*Pair up each word with one from the box below. Then say what is the*
*connection between them. The first one is done for you.*

a)  nūntius    nūntiat    messenger    announces

b)  bēstia     _____    _____

c)  mors       _____    _____

d)  pugna      _____    _____

e)  clāmor     _____    _____

f)  gladiātor  _____    _____

| clāmat   nūntiat   bēstiārius   mortuus   pugnat   gladius |

3   *Translate this sentence:* spectātor spectāculum spectat. _____

_____

*Why do all these Latin words start in the same way?*

**in amphitheātrō**

*Translate these sentences, taking care with the tenses.*

1  Pompēiānī, postquam amphitheātrum intrāvērunt, bēstiās spectābant.
2  canēs, quod ferōcēs erant, cervōs perterritōs interfēcērunt.
3  postquam lupī canēs facile superāvērunt, spectātōrēs plausērunt.
4  cīvēs erant īrātī quod bēstiāriī leōnēs nōn petīvērunt.
5  cīvēs bēstiāriōs ignāvōs vituperāvērunt quod ex arēnā fugiēbant.

**8.4**  **pāstor et leō**

1  *Complete each sentence by using a group of words from the box below. Then translate the sentence into English.*

| | |
|---|---|
| bēstiās vīdit | eum nōn cōnsūmpsit |
| quam celerrimē extrāxit | spīnam īnspexit |
| et eum ad arēnam dūxērunt | |

a)  pāstor, quod benignus erat, _____.

b)  pāstor spīnam _____.

c)  Rōmānī hunc pāstōrem comprehendērunt _____.

_____.

d)  pāstor, postquam arēnam intrāvit, _____.

e)  leō, postquam pāstōrem olfēcit, _____.

2  *The Latin word* **pēs**, **pedem** *(foot) gives us many words in English. Write one of these next to the definitions below. The first one is done for you.*

a)  A person who is travelling on **foot**.     pedestrian

b)  A **foot** or base for a statue.          _____

c)  A creature with 100 **feet**.            _____

d)  A creature with 1000 **feet**.           _____

e)  A bicycle part for the **feet**.          _____

f)  Get under someone's **feet**, hinder.      _____

**bēstiae**

*Complete the following sentences with the correct forms of the words in boldface and then translate the sentences into English.*

---

1  **lupus, lupum, lupī, lupōs**

ingēns _____ ululāvit et per silvam festīnāvit.

---

2  **aper, aprum, aprī, aprōs**

_____ ferōcēs in monte latēbant. iuvenēs _____ saepe agitābant.

---

3  **cervus, cervum, cervī, cervōs**

_____ arēnam intrāvērunt. gladiātōrēs _____ facile superāvērunt.

---

4  **leō, leōnem, leōnēs**

_____ lacrimābat quod pēs dolēbat. pāstor _____ audīvit.

---

5  **serpēns, serpentem, serpentēs**

_____ in pecūniā iacēbat. avārus _____ laudāvit quod servus optimus erat.

---

6  **pāvō, pāvōnem, pāvōnēs**

_____ in hortō clāmōrem faciēbant. servī _____ audīvērunt.

---

**56**

# Which is the correct accusative?

*Look at the first picture. Your teacher will read out two sentences, A and B.*
*Which sentence describes the picture accurately? Put A or B in the box beside the*
*picture. Then do the rest of the exercise in the same way.*

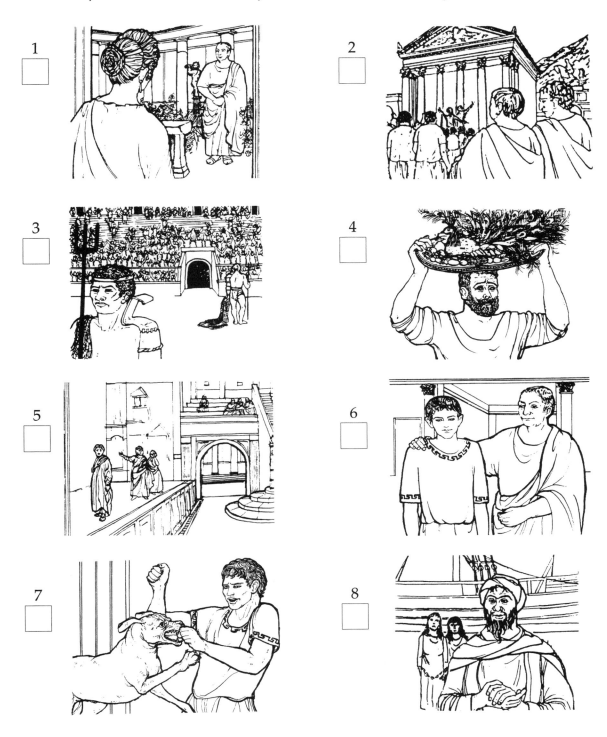

1

2

3

4

5

6

7

8

**Audīte / Dīcite**

A *and* B *alternate reading each sentence, asking the question and verifying the partner's response.*

New question words: **quandō** – when? **quo** – where (to)?
**quot** – how many?

**A**

1 vēnālīcius multōs servōs vēndēbat.
quis vēndēbat? (vēnālīcius)

2 ego tubās audiēbam.
quid audiēbam? (tubās)

3 centuriō multōs gladiōs habet.
quid centuriō habet? (gladiōs)

4 mercātor fēminās ad tabernam dūxit.
quās mercātor dūxit? (fēminās)

5 senex īrātissimus servōs vituperābat.
quōs senex vituperābat? (servōs)

6 umbra omnēs puellās terruit.
quid puellās terruit? (umbra)

7 lībertus pōculum ad triclīnium portat.
quō lībertus pōculum portat?
(ad triclīnium)

8 subitō puer centuriōnēs cōnspicit.
quis centuriōnēs cōnspicit? (puer)

9 turba nūntiōs exspectābat.
quid turba agēbat? (exspectābat)

10 pater statim puerōs vocāvit.
quōs pater vocāvit? (puerōs)

11 clāmor īnfantēs in cubiculō terruit.
quōs clāmor terruit? (īnfantēs)

**B**

1 vēnālīcius multōs servōs vēndēbat.
quōs vēndēbat? (multōs servōs)

2 ego tubās audiēbam.
quis audiēbat? (ego)

3 centuriō multōs gladiōs habet.
quot gladiōs centuriō habet? (multōs)

4 mercātor fēminās ad tabernam dūxit.
quō mercātor fēminās dūxit?
(ad tabernam)

5 senex īrātissimus servōs vituperābat.
quid senex agēbat? (vituperābat)

6 umbra omnēs puellās terruit.
quās umbra terruit? (omnēs puellās)

7 lībertus pōculum ad triclīnium portat.
quid lībertus portat? (pōculum)

8 subitō puer centuriōnēs cōnspicit.
quōs puer cōnspicit? (centuriōnēs)

9 turba nūntiōs exspectābat.
quōs turba exspectābat? (nūntiōs)

10 pater statim puerōs vocāvit.
quandō pater puerōs vocāvit? (statim)

11 clāmor īnfantēs in cubiculō terruit.
ubi erant īnfantēs? (in cubiculō)

## 8.8 Superlatives

*In each Latin sentence, circle the adjective or adverb in parentheses which correctly translates the boldface English word or words.*

1 The spectators were **very happy** then.
tum spectātōrēs erant (laetī/laetissimī).

2 The gladiators were **brave**.
gladiātōrēs erant (fortēs/fortissimī).

3 The net-fighter killed the murmillo **as quickly as possible**.
rētiārius murmillōnem (quam celerrimē/celeriter) interfēcit.

4 The wolves killed the dogs **quickly**.
lupī canēs (celerrimē/celeriter) interfēcērunt.

5 You are holding back the **most ferocious** boars.
tū aprōs (ferōcēs/ferōcissimōs) retinēs.

6 Caecilius liked the **very big** picture.
Caecilius pictūram (maximam/magnam) amābat.

7 The picture was expensive, because it was **very beautiful**.
pictūra erat pretiōsa, quod erat (pulchra/pulcherrima).

8 Your dress is **beautiful**.
stola tua est (pulcherrima/pulchra).

9 My dog is **big**.
canis meus est (magnus/maximus).

10 The dogs killed the deer **very quickly**.
canēs cervōs (celeriter/celerrimē) interfēcērunt.

11 Yesterday the ghost was **very angry**.
heri umbra erat (īrātissima/īrāta).

12 Today the ghost is **satisfied**.
hodiē umbra est (contentissima/contenta).

## 8.9 Gladiatorial Shows

*Read pages 134–138 in your textbook and answer the following:*

1  What was one of the most popular Roman entertainments?

2  Where was it held?

3  Give a description of the building.

4  What was the policy on admission fees?

5  When did the games begin?

6  What two things happened before the gladiators arrived?

7  What three things did the gladiators do before they paired off?

8  What types of people might be gladiators?

9  How were they trained?

10  What information do the programs on page 135 give about the fate of the gladiators who lost a fight?

11  How would
a) a gladiator show he had surrendered?
b) spectators show if they wanted a gladiator killed or allowed to live?

12  Who made the final decision for death or mercy?

13  What reasons might there be to allow a gladiator to live?

14  What Latin phrase shows that gladiators were sometimes very popular (page 135)?

15  What was the highest honor for a gladiator?

16  How did the following types of gladiators differ?
a) Samnites          c) Thracians
b) **murmillōnēs**      d) **rētiāriī**

17  List other types of gladiators who might be part of a day's program.

18  What would have helped make the gladiatorial shows brilliant spectacles?

19  Describe the following:
a) **vēnātiō**          b) **bēstiae**          c) **bēstiāriī**

20  Briefly explain the involvement of the following people in the story of the riot in A.D. 59:
a) Tacitus       c) Nero              e) the wounded
b) Regulus       d) the people of Nuceria       f) the Senate

**60**

## 9.1   Who was the original Milo?

*The Greeks and Romans had long told stories about a sports "star" named Milo. This legendary Milo came from the Greek colony of Croton, on the instep of Italy, in the 6th century B.C. The following is an account of the best-known episode in the original Milo's long athletic career and ends with a brief description of his unusually violent death.*

### luctātor Milō

Milō erat āthlēta Graecus. Milō erat luctātor fortissimus. sexiēs in lūdīs Olympicīs, sexiēs in lūdīs Pȳthiīs erat victor. Milō erat nōtissimus, et omnēs Graecī hērōem laudāvērunt.

   hic āthlēta saepe in palaestrā sē exercēbat. cīvēs fābulam mīrābilem dē hōc āthlētā nārrābant: "ōlim Milō taurum dē monte portāvit. hērōs, postquam hunc taurum ūnō ictū necāvit, tōtum taurum cōnsūmpsit." Milō ingentissimus ē palaestrā prōcēdēbat. spectātōrēs, postquam Milōnem vīdērunt, domum contendērunt. fābulam dē taurō fēminīs et servīs nārrābant.

   posteā Milō iterum ad montem prōcessit. ēheu! lupī ferōcissimī Milōnem vīvum cōnsūmpsērunt.

| | | | |
|---|---|---|---|
| luctātor | *wrestler* | ūnō ictū | *with one blow* |
| sexiēs | *six times* | tōtum | *whole* |
| in lūdīs Olympicīs | *in the Olympic games* | domum | *home* |
| in lūdīs Pȳthiīs | *in the Pythian games* | vīvum | *alive* |
| dē | *about* | | |
| taurum | *bull* | | |

## 9.2   Mix and Match

*For each derivative, write the Latin root on the line at the right; then match the definition to the English derivative.*

| | | | |
|---|---|---|---|
| A | quickness, swiftness | ___ 1 revenue | _____ |
| B | a note added as an afterthought | ___ 2 medieval | _____ |
| C | characteristic of the Middle Ages | ___ 3 notorious | _____ |
| D | financial return from an investment | ___ 4 diary | _____ |
| E | widely but unfavorably known | ___ 5 postscript | _____ |
| F | a daily written record | ___ 6 celerity | _____ |

## 9.3 Odd One Out

*In each set of words circle the one which does not belong.*

1 ingēns   parvus   magnus   ferōx
2 caldārium   ātrium   tepidārium   frīgidārium
3 dormiēbat   portābat   contendit   salūtābat
4 cubiculum   sella   lectus   mēnsa
5 clāmat   ululat   pugnat   cantat   lātrat
6 coquus   māter   fīlius   pater   uxor
7 canis   leō   serpēns   cervus   fēlēs
8 amīcīs   ancillīs   nūntiōs   mercātōribus   iuvenibus
9 cēnam   hortum   canem   ancillās   vīllam
10 tablīnum   forum   triclīnium   ātrium   cubiculum
11 theātrum   fābula   gladiātor   scaena   āctor
12 mercātor   uxor   tōnsor   āctor   pictor
13 cibus   stola   tunica   toga   ānulus
14 novācula   strigilis   hortus   gladius   stilus
15 puellae   iuvenēs   senēs   fēmina   puerī
16 hortus   forum   palaestra   larārium   peristȳlium
17 fūstis   vīnum   pānis   bibit   cōnsūmit
18 rētiārius   argentārius   murmillō   bēstiārius   gladiātor
19 stābant   sedēbant   servābant   vocant   dūcēbant
20 ignāvus   nūntius   īrātus   benignus   occupātus

## 9.4 How many words can you find?

1 *Put together as many Latin words as you can,
using only the letters in the following sentence:*
**discus statuam percussit**. (*e.g.* **tum, discit, pater**)

2 Whose statue is this? What is the
connection between this statue and
the word **ōlim**?

# To Whom? For Whom?

*Look at each picture. Read the sentence and mark the correct word in parentheses.*

1  Caecilius (Clēmentī, Syphācī)
pecūniam dedit.

2  Metella (fīliō, canī) togam quaerēbat.

3  Quīntus (amīcīs, lupīs) fābulam
nārrāvit.

4  Caecilius (ancillae, hospitī) vīnum
optimum offerēbat.

5  nūntiī (cīvī, cīvibus) spectāculum
nūntiāvērunt.

6  leō (pāstōribus, pāstōrī) pedem
ostendit.

**63**

**in tabernā**

Caecilius, Metella, and Quintus are going shopping in Pompeii.

1   *Find a partner.*

2   *One of you should play the part of the merchant, the other the part of Caecilius, Metella, or Quintus.*

3   *Choose together ONE thing you want to buy or sell from the box below.*

| tunicam | pōculum | statuam | ānulum | stolam | gladium |

4   *Read through the dialogue below, putting your article and prices in the gaps. A list of possible prices is given below.*

5   *Act the dialogue.*

Merchant:   salvē! quid quaeris?

Shopper:   salvē, mercātor! ego _____ quaerō.

Merchant:   _____ habeō. ecce!

Shopper:   quantī est?

Merchant:   ego _____ dēnāriōs cupiō.

Shopper:   tū _____ dēnāriōs cupis? furcifer! ego tibi

_____ dēnāriōs offerō.

Merchant:   _____ dēnāriōs cupiō.

Shopper:   tibi _____ dēnāriōs offerō.

Merchant:   quid? ego nūllam pecūniam habeō. _____

dēnāriōs cupiō.

Shopper:   tū nimium postulās. ego _____ dēnāriōs dō.

Merchant:   cōnsentiō. ego tibi grātiās maximās agō. valē!

| 10 | decem | 35 | trīgintā quīnque |
| 15 | quīndecim | 40 | quadrāgintā |
| 20 | vīgintī | 45 | quadrāgintā quīnque |
| 25 | vīgintī quīnque | 50 | quīnquāgintā |
| 30 | trīgintā | 55 | quīnquāgintā quīnque |

1 *The small pictures show different parts of the baths. Write each of the following captions underneath the picture to which it belongs.*

> a) Pompēiānī sē exercēbant.
> b) servus dominum rādēbat.
> c) fēmina ad tabernam ambulābat.
> d) iuvenis ad thermās vēnit.
> e) cīvēs togās dēposuērunt.

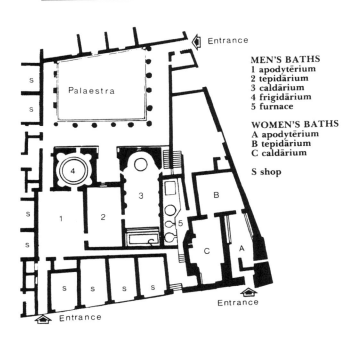

MEN'S BATHS
1 apodytērium
2 tepidārium
3 caldārium
4 frigidārium
5 furnace

WOMEN'S BATHS
A apodytērium
B tepidārium
C caldārium

S shop

1 _____

2 _____

3 _____

4 _____

5 _____

2 *Draw a line from each picture to the right part of the plan.*

**65**

**Seneca's Noisy Neighbors**

1 *Seneca wrote about the noise near his home in Rome. Here are some Latin words from his description. As you read through the passage, put the correct letter in the parentheses.*

| A audiō | B clāmor | C sē exercent | D saliunt |
|---------|----------|---------------|-----------|
| E fūr | F numquam tacet | G habitō | H omnēs |

"Uproar ( ) surrounds me. I live ( ) over a set of baths. Just imagine the babel of sounds that strikes my ears. When the **athletic gentlemen** below are exercising themselves ( ), lifting lead weights, I can hear their grunts. I hear ( ) the whistling of their breath as it escapes from their lungs. I can hear somebody enjoying a cheap rub down and the smack of the masseur's hands on his shoulders. If his hand comes down flat, it makes one sound; if it comes down hollowed, it makes another. Add to this the noise when a brawler or **thief** ( ) is being arrested down below, the racket made by the man who likes to sing in his bath or the sound of **enthusiasts** who jump ( ) into the water with a tremendous splash. Next, I can hear the screech of the hair-plucker, who advertises himself by shouting. He is never quiet ( ) except when he is plucking hair and making his victim shout instead. Finally, just imagine the cries the **sausage-man**, the cake-seller, and all ( ) the other food-sellers make as they advertise their goods, adding to the din."

2 *Seneca describes the following people in the baths. Where would they carry on their activities there? Read the passage again for clues and then mark the correct place.*

a) **athletic gentlemen**: in apodytēriō, in palaestrā, in frīgidāriō
b) **thief**: in forō, in caldāriō, in apodytēriō
c) **enthusiasts**: in caldāriō, in cubiculō, in palaestrā
d) **sausage-man**: in tepidāriō, in triclīniō, in basilicā

3 *Which of these Latin sentences best suits the activities of each individual or group mentioned in 2 above? Put their letter in the parentheses.*

( ) discum ēmittēbant          ( ) magnum clāmōrem faciēbant
( ) cibum offerēbat            ( ) togam cēpit et effūgit

4 *The bold letters in the Latin sentences above make an English word when re-arranged.*

**Clue:** It draws hot air up the sides of a room.

**Answer:** ___ ___ ___ ___

**Audīte / Dīcite**

A *and* B *alternate reading each sentence, asking the question, and verifying the partner's response.*

New question words: **cui** – to/for whom (sg.)?
**quibus** – to/for whom (pl.)?

**A**

1 fēminae mercātōrī pecūniam dedērunt.
cui fēminae pecūniam dedērunt? (mercātōrī)

2 dominus amīcō cēnam parābat.
quid dominus parābat? (cēnam)

3 iuvenis puellae ānulum ēmit.
quid iuvenis ēmit? (ānulum)

4 senex nūntiīs forum ostendit.
quis forum ostendit? (senex)

5 coquus fēminīs vīnum offerēbat.
quibus coquus vīnum offerēbat? (fēminīs)

6 senex omnibus puerīs fābulam nārrat.
quid agit senex? (fābulam nārrat)

7 pater mihi canem dedit.
cui pater canem dedit? (mihi)

8 servus tibi togam trādidit.
quis togam trādidit? (servus)

9 agricola tibi dōnum offerēbat.
cui agricola dōnum offerēbat? (tibi)

10 tū mihi ānulum emis.
quis emit? (tū)

11 servus centuriōnī gladium trādidit.
quid ēgit servus? (gladium trādidit)

12 poēta cīvibus versum recitābat.
quibus poēta versum recitābat? (cīvibus)

**B**

1 fēminae mercātōrī pecūniam dedērunt.
quid fēminae dedērunt? (pecūniam)

2 dominus amīcō cēnam parābat.
cui dominus cēnam parābat? (amīcō)

3 iuvenis puellae ānulum ēmit.
cui iuvenis ānulum ēmit? (puellae)

4 senex nūntiīs forum ostendit.
quid senex ostendit? (forum)

5 coquus fēminīs vīnum offerēbat.
quid coquus offerēbat? (vīnum)

6 senex omnibus puerīs fābulam nārrat.
quis nārrat? (senex)

7 pater mihi canem dedit.
quis mihi canem dedit? (pater)

8 servus tibi togam trādidit.
quid servus trādidit? (togam)

9 agricola tibi dōnum offerēbat.
quid agricola agēbat? (dōnum offerēbat)

10 tū mihi ānulum emis.
cui ānulum emis? (mihi)

11 servus centuriōnī gladium trādidit.
quis gladium trādidit? (servus)

12 poēta cīvibus versum recitābat.
quid poēta recitābat? (versum)

## 9.10 The Baths

*Read pages 154–158 in your textbook and answer the following:*

1 At what time of day would Caecilius go to the baths?

2 What kinds of activities took place in the baths?

3 Who was the **ōstiārius**?

4 What was the **palaestra**?

5 What three activities did people do there?

6 What did Caecilius do in the following rooms?
   a) **apodytērium**
   b) **tepidārium**
   c) **caldārium**
   d) **frīgidārium**

7 How were oil and strigils used in the baths?

8 What seven types of people did Seneca constantly hear in the baths?

9 From whom did the Romans learn to build baths?

10 What feature of the bath complex did Roman skill improve?

11 Explain how this system worked.

12 Give the name for this system.

13 Where else was the system used?

14 What was the most commonly used fuel for the furnaces?

15 Study the plan on page 158.

# Which is the correct verb?

*In each Latin sentence, circle the verb form in parentheses which is correct.*
*If you cannot remember the correct ending, consult pages 230–232 of your*
*textbook.*

1 ego (sum / sumus) coquus.
  ego cēnam (parāmus / parō).

2 nōs Pompēiānī (sumus / sum) īrātī.
  nōs gladiōs (vibrō / vibrāmus).

3 tū (estis / es) mercātor.
  tū mihi togam (ostendis / ostenditis).

4 vōs Nūcerīnī (es / estis) turbulentī.
  vōs amphitheātrum et omnēs viās (complēs / complētis).

5 ego (sumus / sum) ancilla.
  ego suāviter (cantō / cantāmus).

6 tū (es / estis) gladiātor.
  tū pecūniam (postulātis / postulās).

# Who is bigger?  Who is smaller?

*First study the picture on this page and then*
*mark it according to instructions.*

1 Mark an "x" under the picture of
  the **iuvenis** who is **maior**.
2 Mark a "y" under the picture of
  the **puella** who is **minor**.

# Creative Comparatives

*On a separate sheet of paper, write FIVE Latin sentences using words in section **A** and 5 Latin sentences using words in section **B**. To compose a Latin sentence, choose one word from column 1, one from 3, and one from 5. Then translate each sentence.*

For example,

| 1 | 2 | 3 | 4 | 5 | |
|---|---|---|---|---|---|
| āthlēta | est | nōtior | quam | coquus. | The athlete is more famous than the cook. |

## Section A

| 1 | 2 | 3 | 4 | 5 |
|---|---|---|---|---|
| dominus | est | ferōcior | quam | dominus |
| fēmina | | fortior | | ego |
| frāter | | ingentior | | fēmina |
| hospes | | maior | | frāter |
| ille homō | | nōtior | | hospes |
| iuvenis | | pulchrior | | ille homō |
| puella | | minor | | iuvenis |
| puer | | | | puella |
| uxor | | | | puer |
| | | | | tū |
| | | | | uxor |

## Section B

| 1 | 2 | 3 | 4 | 5 |
|---|---|---|---|---|
| ancillae | sunt | ferōciōrēs | quam | ancillae |
| āthlētae | | fortiōrēs | | āthlētae |
| caupōnēs | | ingentiōrēs | | caupōnēs |
| coquī | | maiōrēs | | coquī |
| gladiātōrēs | | nōtiōrēs | | gladiātōrēs |
| illī hominēs | | pulchriōrēs | | illī hominēs |
| pistōrēs | | minōrēs | | nōs |
| rhētorēs | | | | pistōrēs |
| vēnāliciī | | | | rhētorēs |
| | | | | vēnāliciī |
| | | | | vōs |

**What's going on?**

*Your teacher will read a sentence to you with the verb omitted. Underline the verb which completes the sentence correctly. The first two have pictures to help you.*

1    laudant   aedificant   vocant  _____

2    surgunt   cōnsūmunt   audiunt  _____

3    habitābat   vidēbat   pulsābat  _____

4    contendimus   bibimus   pingimus  _____

5    dedit   cōnspexit   scrīpsit  _____

6    pugnātis   lacrimātis   intrātis  _____

7    terreō   ostendō   sedeō  _____

8    revenīs   spectās   curris  _____

9    habēbat   manēbat   respondēbat  _____

10   intellēxērunt   rīsērunt   fēcērunt  _____

**contentiō**

*The following is an argument between a Greek (G) and a Roman (R). Complete the sentences with words from the box below. Then, working with a partner, read the sentences as a dialogue.*

| | | | | |
|---|---|---|---|---|
| docēmus | pingimus | estis | aedificāmus | sumus |
| spectātis | accipitis | audītis | servāmus | facimus |
| pugnātis | habētis | superāmus | labōrāmus | |

R   nōs Rōmānī viās et pontēs _____.

G   sed nōs Graecī statuās _____. nōs pictūrās _____.

R   vōs semper āctōrēs _____. vōs estis ignāvī. nōs Rōmānī

   dīligenter _____.

G   vōs estis barbarī quod semper _____.

R   vos _____ turbulentī quod semper contentiōnēs

   _____. nōs Rōmānī pācem _____.

G   sed vōs semper praemium _____.

R   nōs Rōmānī _____ fortissimī. nōs Graecōs semper

   _____.

G   vōs tamen rhētorēs Graecōs _____. nōs Graecī Rōmānōs

   _____. nōs sumus auctōrēs.

# Word Equations

*Each of the following formulae represents a derivative from the Vocabulary Checklist. Combine the prefixes and/or suffixes (in capital letters) with the Latin root suggested by the English word in lower-case letters to form the derivative. Watch for simple spelling changes in the roots.*

1   OB + save + NT   _____

2   lonely + TUDE   _____

3   E + announce + ATE   _____

4   RE + take + TURE   _____

5   always + TERNAL   _____

## 10.7 Comparisons

*Here are some adjectives with their comparatives and superlatives. Pick the most suitable adjectives to complete the Latin captions to the pictures. Look carefully at the three pictures before you choose.*

| | | | | | |
|---|---|---|---|---|---|
| doctus | doctior | doctissimus | longus | longior | longissimus |
| sordida | sordidior | sordidissima | nōtus | nōtior | nōtissimus |
| īrātus | īrātior | īrātissimus | | | |

 Milō est nōtior.

Caecilius est nōtus.

 Iūlius Caesar est _____ .

 Thrasymachus est _____ .

 Diodōrus est īrātior.

 Alexander est _____ .

 hic liber est _____ .

 hic liber est _____ .

 hic liber est _____ .

 haec stola est _____ .

 haec stola est _____ .

 haec stola est _____ .

 rhētor est _____ .

 iuvenis est _____ .

 puer est _____ .

73

# Teach yourself Greek

**1** *Greek was one of the subjects students would learn in a Roman school. They would start by learning the letters of the alphabet and their correct pronunciation. Look at the alphabet. How many letters do you recognize? Which ones would you have to learn?*

| Form | Name | English equivalent |
|------|------|--------------------|
| A α | Alpha | a |
| B β | Beta | b |
| Γ γ | Gamma | g (as in *g*ood) |
| Δ δ | Delta | d |
| E ε | Epsilon | e (as in g*e*t) |
| Z ζ | Zeta | zd (as in wi*sd*om) |
| H η | Eta | ē (as in h*ai*r) |
| Θ θ | Theta | th (as in *th*eater) |
| I ι | Iota | i |
| K κ | Kappa | k |
| Λ λ | Lambda | l |
| M μ | Mu | m |
| N ν | Nu | n |
| Ξ ξ | Xi | x |
| O o | Omicron | o (as in g*o*t) |
| Π π | Pi | p |
| P ρ | Rho | r (ῥ = rh) |
| Σ σ, ς | Sigma | s (ς is used at the end of words) |
| T τ | Tau | t |
| Y υ | Upsilon | u |
| Φ φ | Phi | ph |
| X χ | Chi | ch (as in *ch*orus) |
| Ψ ψ | Psi | ps |
| Ω ω | Omega | ō (as in sh*ow*) |

There is no letter *h* in Greek. To show the sound *h* at the beginning of a word the Greeks used the sign ʽ over a vowel, e.g. ὁδός (a road) pronounced hodos. Words that begin with a vowel but do not have the h sound, have the sign ʼ over the vowel, e.g. ἐν (in) pronounced en.

**2** *The following Greek words are still used in English. What are they? You may have to make a few small changes in spelling.*

| Greek | English | Greek | English |
|-------|---------|-------|---------|
| ΚΟΜΜΑ | _____ | δράμα | _____ |
| ΙΡΙΣ | _____ | ἠχώ | _____ |
| ΚΡΑΤΗΡ | _____ | πάνθηρ | _____ |
| ΟΡΙΖΩΝ | _____ | ἄσθμα | _____ |
| ΚΡΙΣΙΣ | _____ | νέκταρ | _____ |
| ΙΔΕΑ | _____ | ῥοδόδενδρον | _____ |
| ΧΑΟΣ | _____ | μανία | _____ |
| ΚΙΝΗΜΑ | _____ | ὀρχήστρα | _____ |
| ΑΣΒΕΣΤΟΣ | _____ | ἱπποπόταμος | _____ |
| ΧΑΡΑΚΤΗΡ | _____ | καταστροφή | _____ |

**3** *Some of the characters in the stories have Greek names. Look at the list below and write down their names in Latin.*

| Greek | Latin | Greek | Latin |
|-------|-------|-------|-------|
| Μελισσα | _____ | Παντάγαθος | _____ |
| Θεόδωρος | _____ | Ἑρμογενής | _____ |
| Θρασύμαχος | _____ | Ἀλέξανδρος | _____ |

Which of these names are still used today in English with little or no change? _____

Here are a few more Greek names that are also used today in English.

Ζωή, Φίλιππος, Δάφνη, Ἑλένη, Πέτρος, Γεωργός

**4** *The Greek words below were used in Latin before they came into English. First change the Greek letters into the Roman alphabet, then write down the matching Latin and English words.*

| Greek | Roman alphabet | Latin word | English word |
|-------|----------------|------------|--------------|
| Θέατρον | _____ | _____ | _____ |
| δίσκος | _____ | _____ | _____ |
| φιλόσοφος | _____ | _____ | _____ |
| Θέρμαι | _____ | _____ | _____ |
| στολή | _____ | _____ | _____ |
| σκηνή | _____ | _____ | _____ |

**Writing Materials**

*What are the writing materials below made of? Choose the right substances from the box below and write them down in the appropriate space below the picture. Some of the articles could be made from more than one substance.*

| feather | wax | plastic | aluminum | resin | reed |
|---------|-----|---------|----------------|-------|--------|
| wood | ivory | soot | stainless steel | bone | bronze |

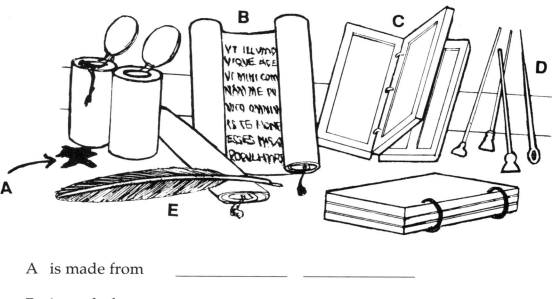

A   is made from   _____   _____

B   is made from   _____

C   is made from   _____   _____

D   is made from   _____   _____   _____

E   is made from   _____

*What three substances in the box above were not used by the Romans?*

*Why not?*

## 10.10 Audīte / Dīcite

*A and B alternate reading the sentences aloud, supplying the Latin pronoun that tells who is doing the action, and verifying the partner's response.*

| A | B |
|---|---|
| 1  pictōrēs sumus. | 1  *nōs* pictōrēs sumus. |
| 2  *ego* nunc cibum parō. | 2  nunc cibum parō. |
| 3  tabernam intrō. | 3  *ego* tabernam intrō. |
| 4  quid *tū* vidēs? | 4  quid vidēs? |
| 5  cūr in palaestrā pugnās? | 5  cūr *tū* in palaestrā pugnās? |
| 6  quī *vōs* estis? | 6  quī estis? |
| 7  per viās ambulāmus. | 7  *nōs* per viās ambulāmus. |
| 8  *ego* pauper sum. | 8  pauper sum. |
| 9  canem vituperātis. | 9  *vōs* canem vituperātis. |
| 10  *nōs* nūntiōs vidēmus. | 10  nūntiōs vidēmus. |

## 10.11 Education

*Read pages 175–178 in your textbook and answer the following:*

1 Describe pre-school learning for most Roman children.

2 At what age was formal schooling usually begun?

3 To what extent were Roman schools coeducational?

4 Describe the education of an upper-class Roman girl.

5 How many students and how many teachers were there in the first school a Roman child would attend?

6 What was the name of the first teacher a Roman child would have?

7 What did a typical Roman classroom look like?

8 Did Roman children have to attend school?

9 Was there an educational fee?

10 Why would children go to school?

11 What were the duties of a **paedagōgus**?

**Education (continued)**

12  What three things did children study with the **lūdī magister**?

13  What are the definitions of these terms?
    a) **tabulae**    b) **stilus**    c) **papȳrus**

14  What instruments were used for writing on papyrus?

15  What was ink made from?

16  How did the students work in school?

17  What was classroom discipline like?

18  How long was a school day?

19  When did the students have holidays?

20  When did Quintus go to secondary school?

21  What was his teacher's name at this level?

22  For what works were the following authors famous?
    a)  Homer            b)  Aeschylus           c)  Vergil
                            Sophocles               Horace
                            Euripides

23  What was the major way to study the works of these men besides listening and reciting the pieces?

24  What two other subjects were taught? For what reason were they taught?

25  When would Quintus leave the **grammaticus**?

26  What two languages would he know well?

27  Why was it important for him to know Greek?

28  Who was the teacher at the third level of education?

29  What two things did he teach?

30  In what three ways would a Roman use the skills gained in this school?

31  When the rhetor taught public speaking, what were four parts to this training?

32  a)  What was the purpose of ordinary Roman schools?
    b)  What four abilities did this include?

33  How did a student learn (a) science or (b) technical skills?

**Whom does he support?**

**magna turba est in forō, quod multī cīvēs candidātōs inspiciunt.**

*In each Latin sentence below, circle the noun in parentheses that correctly translates the English words in boldface.*

1a  The sailor greets **the farmer**.
nauta (agricolam / agricolae) salūtat.

1b  The sailor gives his support **to the farmer**.
nauta (agricolam / agricolae) favet.

2a  The barber greets **the baker**.
tōnsor (pistōrī / pistōrem) salūtat.

2b  The barber has faith **in the baker**.
tōnsor (pistōrī / pistōrem) crēdit.

3a  The young man greets **his candidate**; the candidate is an athlete.
iuvenis (candidātō / candidātum) salūtat; candidātus est āthlēta.

3b  The young man has faith **in the athlete**.
iuvenis (āthlētae / āthlētam) crēdit.

4a  The thief greets a **very bad candidate**; the candidate is a thief too.
fūr (candidātum pessimum / candidātō pessimō) salūtat; candidātus quoque est fūr.

4b  The candidate gives **the thief** a club.
candidātus (fūrem / fūrī) fūstem dat.

# Which word does not belong?

*In each of these groups of words, circle the one that is not associated with the word in boldface.*

1 **culīna**
cēna
cibus
coquus
pāstor
pāvō

2 **theātrum**
āctor
fābula
scaena
spectātōrēs
vīlla

3 **vēnālīcius**
ancilla
nāvis
portus
servī
tuba

4 **versipellis**
lupus
pulcher
silva
tunica
ululāvit

5 **cēna**
bibit
cōnsūmit
lectus
tablīnum
triclīnium

6 **arēna**
avārī
canēs
cervī
leōnēs
lupī

7 **basilica**
accūsat
canis
cēra
iūdex
signum

8 **Graecī**
barbarī
philosophī
pictōrēs
rhētorēs
sculptōrēs

# What is the meaning?

*The words in the sentences below have been put in various orders which are new to you. Write a translation for each sentence on a separate sheet of paper.*

1 servus quaerēbat gladium murmillōnī.
2 nārrāvērunt fābulam fīliīs fēminae.
3 rētiāriīs Rēgulus dedit signum.
4 spectāculum nūntiāvērunt cīvibus nūntiī.
5 mercātōrī dedit dēnāriōs fēmina.

**Derivative Crux**

*You may use a dictionary.*

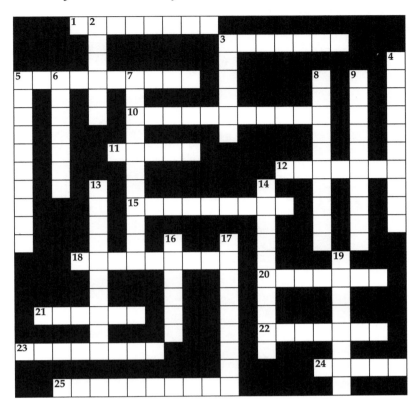

**ACROSS**

1 belief as to the truth of something (crēdit)
3 a community, especially of nuns (convenit)
5 pertaining to a senator (senātor)
10 farewell speech (valē)
11 statement of beliefs (crēdit)
12 least possible (minimē)
15 predatory (rapit)
18 unable to be read (legit)
20 to assemble (convenit)
21 table on a map which explains the symbols (legit)
22 usefulness (ūtilis)
23 to cause to appear foolish (stultus)
24 of greatest importance (prīmus)
25 containing a promise (as in an IOU) (prōmittit)

**DOWN**

2 animal which preys on other animals (rapit)
3 trustworthiness (as in financial matters) (crēdit)
4 generosity (līberālis)
5 anxious or concerned (sollicitus)
6 a favorite, but unproven, remedy or cure (noster)
7 to re-echo (verberat)
8 an assembly (convenit)
9 involving members of a single school (mūrus)
13 too pleased with oneself (placet)
14 inclined to fight (pugna)
16 having a strong, masculine spirit (vir)
17 politeness, refinement (gēns)
19 of the third rank (tertius)

**Questions and Answers**

*Your teacher will read out a series of questions in Latin. Decide which of the people or things below answers each question. Put the question number in the box next to the picture letter.*

a)

b)

c)

d)

e)

f)

g)

h)

i)

## 11.6 Graffiti

1 *These graffiti were found on walls in Pompeii. What do they mean?*

a) Aemilius Celer hīc habitat

b) Marcus Spedūsa amat

c) Nūcerīnīs īnfēlīcia!

d) fūr, cavē!

e) Minūcī, murmillō, valē!

f) Restitūtus multās saepe puellās dēcēpit

2 *What does the label below say?*

Rūfus est

| | |
|---|---|
| hīc | *here* |
| īnfēlīcia | *bad luck* |
| Minūcī | *Minucius* |
| dēcēpit | *has deceived* |

3 *Some of the writers of graffiti made mistakes. Find a mistake in the examples above.*

4 *Choose* TWO *of the graffiti above and write down who you think wrote them and why.*

LABYRINTHVS
HICHABITAT
MIN                OTAVRVS

5 *This drawing of a maze was also found on a wall in Pompeii. It shows the original style of writing. What does it say?*

**Clue:** There's a monster about!

# Once Over Lightly

*Below are some words that have occurred only once or twice in the Stages. Write V or F beside each description. Correct the descriptions which you have marked as F.*

1

2

**tepidārium** ☐            **vēnātiō** ☐

3  **aedīlis**: a slave who took his master's children to school. ☐

4  **hypocaust**: a word used by archaeologists to describe burnt objects. ☐

5  **manumission**: the act of making a slave free. ☐

6  **dēnārius**: a gladiator armed with a net and trident. ☐

7  **duovirī**: the officials who judged cases in the basilica. ☐

8  **tabulae**: wax tablets used for notes, letters and wills. ☐

9  **Herculāneum**: the name given to any picture or statue of Hercules. ☐

10  **penātēs**: gods who were thought to protect a Roman household and to look after the store cupboard. ☐

11  **Campānia**: the area in Italy surrounding Pompeii. ☐

12  **peristȳlium**: the exercise ground at the baths. ☐

13  **ōstiārius**: a candidate's supporter. ☐

14  **alumnī**: slaves acquired as small children. ☐

15  **dīvīsor**: person who distributes election bribes. ☐

## 11.8 Local Government and Elections

*Read pages 194–198 in your textbook and answer the following:*

1   When were elections in Pompeii held?

2   How did people react to the elections?

3   Who were **fautōrēs**?

4   What were the main ways to advertise for a candidate?

5   What offices did candidates run for annually?

6   What were the two main duties of the senior pair?

7   List the eight duties of the junior pair.

8   Who composed the town council?

9   How were these members selected?

10   How did one recognize a candidate?

11   What does **candidus** mean?

12   What three roles did an agent play in the campaign?

13   What illegal form of persuasion was widely practiced?

14   What were legal forms of persuasion?

15   What was expected if a candidate won?

16   How else was a candidate expected to contribute from his own wealth?

17   What was special about these families?
   a)   the Holconii
   b)   the Flacci

18   How did public service affect small towns like Pompeii?

19   As a result, what was an indispensable qualification for taking part in government?

20   What were four advantages of public service?

21   What Roman characteristic made these rewards appealing?

22   When might the central government intervene in local politics?

23   What happened in A.D. 60 in Pompeii? Why?

24   What was a **praefectus**?

**Local Government and Elections (continued)**

25 How long was it before the Pompeians could run their own affairs again?

26 Who were **vīcīnī**?

27 What other groups might support a particular candidate?

28 Who were allowed to vote?

29 Where did they vote?

30 What role did women play in political campaigns?

31 At what time of day were election notices painted on walls?

32 For what two reasons were they done that way?

M·HOLCONIVM
PRISCVM·II·VIR

33 Here is part of one of Holconius' election slogans. What office is he standing for?

**Perfect your tenses.**

*Write the number of each present tense verb in column A in front of its perfect tense equivalent in column B. Translate column B into English.*

| A | | B | Translation |
|---|---|---|---|
| *(1st person sg. & pl. present)* | | *(1st person sg. & pl. perfect)* | |
| 1 abeō | ____ | sēnsī | _____ |
| 2 āmittō | ____ | tacuimus | _____ |
| 3 capiō | ____ | āmīsī | _____ |
| 4 damus | ____ | revēnimus | _____ |
| 5 īnspicimus | ____ | abiī | _____ |
| 6 revenīmus | ____ | dedimus | _____ |
| 7 sentiō | ____ | cēpī | _____ |
| 8 tacēmus | ____ | īnspeximus | _____ |

| A | | B | Translation |
|---|---|---|---|
| *(2nd person sg. & pl. present)* | | *(2nd person sg. & pl. perfect)* | |
| 9 agitās | ____ | recubuistī | _____ |
| 10 cōnspicitis | ____ | cōnsūmpsistī | _____ |
| 11 cōnsūmis | ____ | cōnspexistis | _____ |
| 12 contenditis | ____ | scrīpsistis | _____ |
| 13 dūcis | ____ | contendistis | _____ |
| 14 petitis | ____ | agitāvistī | _____ |
| 15 recumbis | ____ | petīvistis | _____ |
| 16 scrībitis | ____ | dūxistī | _____ |

**Getting Personal**

*Your teacher will read out a verb in English. Circle the corresponding form in Latin.*

| | | | |
|---|---|---|---|
| 1 | prōmīsī | prōmīsistī | prōmīsit |
| 2 | rapiēbās | rapiēbam | rapiēbat |
| 3 | sentiēbat | sentiēbam | sentiēbās |
| 4 | pulsāvimus | pulsāvistis | pulsāvērunt |
| 5 | īnspiciēbant | īnspiciēbāmus | īnspiciēbātis |
| 6 | bibī | bibistī | bibit |
| 7 | dormīvimus | dormīvērunt | dormīvistis |
| 8 | terruistī | terruit | terruī |

*How many of the verbs you have marked are in the perfect tense?*
*How many of the verbs you have marked are in the imperfect tense?*

# The volcano awakes.

*Look at the pictures and read the questions below them. Choose suitable answers from the box below and put them in the space provided.*

| minimē Sulla ita vērō in portū servōs vēndēbat cinerem |

1

ubi erant Syphāx et Celer?

_____

2

cūr Syphāx prope portum stābat?

_____

3

num Poppaea et Lucriō erant laetī?

_____

4

quid sēnsit Lucriō?

_____

5

quis ad Marcum et Quārtum contendit?

_____

6

erantne frātrēs sollicitī?

_____

## 12.4　The Common Denominator

*In each of these groups, circle the word that is not connected with the other words. In the blank provided, give a Latin word that is the common denominator for the remaining words.*

**For example:**

    vīlla      1  ātrium  (tōnsor)  culīna  cubiculum  peristȳlium  tablīnum

_____  2  triclīnium  coquus  larārium  recumbit  bibit  hospes

_____  3  via  mūrus  portus  taberna  imperium  urbs

_____  4  nāvis  mercātor  statua  argentārius  templum

_____  5  labōrat  līberat  deus  lībertus  vēnālīcius  dominus

_____  6  umbra  lūna  versipellis  stēlla  dormit  canis

_____  7  murmillō  arēna  bēstia  stola  pugnat  gladius

_____  8  flamma  cinis  nūbēs  sonus  hortus  tremor

_____  9  stilus  cibus  cēra  liber  contrōversia  sententia

_____ 10  duovir  favet  uxor  titulus  scrīptor  crēdit

_____ 11  fundus  caldārium  palaestra  strigilis  apodytērium togam dēpōnit

## 12.5　Vesuvius

*The picture on the left shows Vesuvius as it appears on a wall-painting excavated in Pompeii. The other pictures show it as it was after the eruption in A.D. 79 and as it is today. Look at the pictures and describe what has happened to Vesuvius in the last two thousand years.*

Before the eruption      After the eruption      Today

# The Last Days of Pompeii

*Complete the account with English words derived from Latin words in the list below. Each one is numbered to help you.*

On August 24, A.D. 79 Mount Vesuvius ¹ _____ with great

² _____. The volcano which had lain ³ _____ for

many years, suddenly awoke. The day before the people had felt earth

⁴ _____ and ⁵ _____ that disaster was

⁶ _____. Soon the ⁷ _____ ⁸ _____

were causing ⁹ _____ problems and thicker ash was

¹⁰ _____ on the town. Some ¹¹ _____ in the

¹² _____ and others ¹³ _____ as they were

trampled by the crowds. Many ¹⁴ _____ refused to flee but

their hopes were ¹⁵ _____ and soon they

¹⁶ _____ as buildings collapsed in ¹⁷ _____

around them. The ¹⁸ _____ scene was one of

¹⁹ _____ devastation and the survivors asked themselves

whether they were victims of a terrible ²⁰ _____ or a

punishment from the gods.

| | | | |
|---|---|---|---|
| 1 | ērumpit (perfect: ērūpit): *breaks out* | 11 | perit: *dies* |
| 2 | violentia: *force* | 12 | flamma: *tongue of fire* |
| 3 | dormit: *sleeps* | 13 | exspīrat: *dies* |
| 4 | tremor: *shaking* | 14 | obstinātē: *stubbornly* |
| 5 | sentit (perfect: sēnsit): *feels* | 15 | frūstrā: *in vain* |
| 6 | imminet: *hangs over, threatens* | 16 | dēspērat: *is without hope* |
| 7 | dēnsus: *thick* | 17 | ruīna: *fallen building* |
| 8 | fūmus: *smoke* | 18 | fīnis: *end* |
| 9 | respīrat: *breathes* | 19 | tōtus: *whole* |
| 10 | dēscendit: *comes down* | 20 | accidit: *happens* |

**Word Search**

| V | E | S | U | V | I | U | S |
|---|---|---|---|---|---|---|---|
|   |   |   |   |   |   |   |   |
|   |   |   |   |   |   |   |   |
|   |   |   |   |   |   |   |   |
|   |   |   |   |   |   |   |   |
|   |   |   |   |   |   |   |   |
|   |   |   |   |   |   |   |   |
|   |   |   |   |   |   |   |   |
|   |   |   |   |   |   |   |   |

Construct your own Latin word search, using the grid provided. Put in only words referring to people or things in the picture above. If you are not sure of a Latin word, look back at the stories and the Vocabulary Checklist in Stage 12.

Use CAPITAL letters in the grid. Keep a list of the Latin words you have included on a separate sheet. Then try your word search out on a friend.

**Audīte / Dīcite**

A *and* B *alternate reading the Latin sentences aloud, supplying the correct pronoun from the parentheses, translating the sentences into English, and verifying the partner's selections and translations.*

**A**

1  (ego / tū) forum intrābās.

2  *nōs* cēnam optimam cupīvimus.
   (We wanted an excellent dinner.)

3  (tū / vōs) librum tuum invēnistis?

4  *ego* īnfantēs spectāvī.
   (I watched the babies.)

5  ēheu! (ego / nōs) pecūniam āmīsī!

6  *vōs* servō epistulās dedistis.
   (You (pl.) gave the slave the letters.)

7  (tū / nōs) maiōrēs flammās vīdimus.

8  *ego* nūbēs spectābam.
   (I was watching the clouds.)

9  (dominus / vōs) hospitī cēnam
   nūntiābātis.

10  *hospes* pōculum īnspexit.
    (The guest inspected the cup.)

11  (nōs / vōs) prope silvam manēbātis.

12  post fābulam, *vōs* contentī erātis?
    (After the play, were you (pl.)
    satisfied?)

**B**

1  *tū* forum intrābās.
   (You were entering the forum.)

2  (tū / nōs) cēnam optimam cupīvimus.

3  *vōs* librum tuum invēnistis?
   (Did you (pl.) find your book?)

4  (ego/nōs) īnfantēs spectāvī.

5  ēheu! *ego* pecūniam āmīsī!
   (Oh no! I lost the money!)

6  (ego / vōs) servō epistulās dedistis.

7  *nōs* maiōrēs flammās vīdimus.
   (We saw bigger flames.)

8  (ego / tū) nūbēs spectābam.

9  *vōs* hospitī cēnam nūntiābātis.
   (You (pl.) were announcing a dinner
   to the guest.)

10  (hospes / ego) pōculum īnspexit.

11  *vōs* prope silvam manēbātis.
    (You (pl.) were staying near the forest.)

12  post fābulam, (ego / vōs) contentī
    erātis?

## 12.9 The Destruction and Excavation of Pompeii

*Read pages 216–220 in your textbook and answer the following:*

1 On what day in A.D. 79 did Mount Vesuvius erupt?

2 Why was the eruption unexpected?

3 What specifically happened to Herculaneum?

4 What specifically happened to Pompeii?

5 What did most people do? Why?

6 What happened to the others?

7 What did the area look like on August 26, A.D. 79?

8 What did the survivors try to do?

9 What happened to the former residents?

10 What eventually happened to the site?

11 What was known about Pompeii in the Middle Ages?

12 When were the first remains found? By whom? What was he doing?

13 What did this man think he had found?

14 Who was Charles III? What did he have to do with the site?

15 In what year did excavators finally realize that they were exploring the lost city of Pompeii?

16 Why were excavations more difficult at Herculaneum?

17 How did excavation methods improve over time?

18 What kind of objects were sent to the National Museum in Naples?

19 What happened to the rest of the items?

20 When archaeologists find a hollow space in the ash, what do they do with it? What is the result?

21 As a result of this process, what remains have been discovered?

22 What is the difference in objects found at Herculaneum compared to those found at Pompeii? Why?

23 How much of Pompeii has been excavated? Herculaneum?

24 What is the amazing fact about the new houses that are found?

# The Eruption of Vesuvius: An Eye-Witness Account

*A young man called Pliny saw the eruption from his uncle's villa at Misenum. His uncle had set out in a boat to rescue some friends near Pompeii. Pliny describes what happened to himself and his mother while they awaited his uncle's return.*

## The Eruption Begins

After my uncle set off, I spent the rest of the day studying. Then I had a bath, ate my dinner, and went to bed. But I didn't get much sleep! We'd been having small earth tremors for some days. They didn't bother us much as we are used to them in Campania, but that night they were bad. Things didn't just shake; they were nearly turned upside-down! I was just getting out of bed to wake my mother when she came bursting into my bedroom to wake me. There's a small courtyard between our house and the sea, so we went and sat down there. I don't know whether to call it courage or stupidity – I was only seventeen at the time – but I asked for my book and I carried on reading and taking notes just as if nothing was the matter. Up came a friend of my uncle's who had recently come to stay with him. When he saw us sitting there and me actually reading, he told us off – me for being foolhardy and my mother for allowing it. I paid no attention and just carried on reading.

Now it was the first hour of the day, and the light was dim and faint. All the buildings around us were tottering, and although we were in an open space, it was so narrow that there was every danger that they would crash down on us. In the end we decided to escape from the town.

## Chaos

When we were clear of the buildings, we stopped to get our breath back. There we had some strange and frightening experiences. We had ordered carriages to be brought out for us. They were on dead level ground, but even so they kept moving backwards and forwards. We tried wedging stones under their wheels, but they wouldn't stay still. Then we saw the sea sucked into itself as if the earthquake had thrown it back. At any rate it had left the sea-bed exposed, and many sea creatures were stranded on dry sand! Inland there was a terrible black cloud. It was broken by flashing, jagged blasts of flame and yawned open to reveal long tongues of fire. It was like lightning in a thunder cloud – but on a vaster scale.

Then our friend started again in a sharper and more urgent tone. "If your brother, your uncle, is still alive, I'm sure he wants you to be safe. If he's dead, he would want you to survive: so why are you hanging around and not escaping?" We told him that we wouldn't start thinking of our own safety until we knew what had happened to my uncle. He didn't stop to argue but ran away from the danger as fast as his legs would carry him.

It wasn't long before that cloud I've told you about came down to the earth and covered the sea, swallowing up Capreae and blotting out the headland of Misenum. My mother began begging me, urging me, ordering me to escape as best I could. "You're a young man," she said. "You can escape, but I'm old and slow. I don't mind dying – so long as I don't cause your death too."

I replied that I would not save myself unless she came too. I took hold of her hand and forced her to go forward step by step. She reluctantly agreed and blamed herself for slowing me down.

## Darkness

At this point there was a shower of ash, but still not a heavy one. I looked back. Behind us a dense black cloud was getting nearer and nearer.

"Let's get off the road," I cried, "while we can still see. Otherwise we'll be knocked down by the crowds following us and get trampled in the darkness."

We'd hardly found a place to sit when the darkness fell. It wasn't the darkness of a moonless or cloudy night – it was the darkness of an inner room when the lamp goes out. Women were shrieking, babies wailing, men shouting. Children were calling for their parents, parents for their children, wives for their husbands. They were trying to recognize each other by the sound of their voices.

Then there was a glimmer of light, but it wasn't daylight. It was the first flickering of the approaching fire. However, it kept away from us and complete darkness came down again, together with a heavy shower of ash. We had to keep getting up to shake it off; otherwise, we would have been buried, crushed under its weight.

## The Light Returns

At last the darkness thinned out and dispersed into smoke and mist. Soon it was real daylight; even the sun broke through, but pale yellow as if it were in eclipse. Still terrified, we saw that everything was changed, buried deep under ash as if under snow. We made our way back to Misenum. There we looked after ourselves as best we could and spent an anxious night wavering between hope and fear. Fear was uppermost as the tremors continued.

But even then, despite the danger we had been through and the danger we saw ahead, we refused to think of escaping until we heard news of my uncle.

*Once you have read the account, answer the following:*

## The Eruption Begins

1  Why did Pliny and his mother not panic when the earth tremors began?
2  Why did they decide to leave the town?

## Chaos

3  Pliny described the effects of the eruption on the land, sea, and sky. What were these effects? Why do you think Pliny chose to write about these particular things?

## Darkness

4  To what did Pliny compare the darkness? What idea of the darkness was he trying to give? What effect did the darkness have on the people?
5  What particular dangers threatened Pliny and his mother at this stage of the eruption?

## The Light Returns

6  What reasons did Pliny and his mother still have to be worried after the darkness dispersed?
7  Look carefully at the map showing the areas affected by falling ash. Does Pliny's account seem to contradict the map?

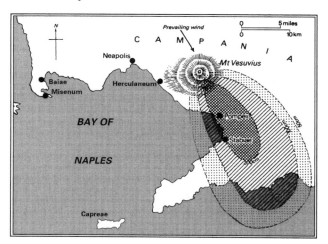

8  Read the whole account again. What impression do you think Pliny wanted to give us of:
   a) his uncle's friend       b) his mother       c) himself?
9  What do *you* think of the way they behaved?
10 Pliny wrote this account many years after the eruption. Do you think his description could still be accurate after such a long time? Give your reasons.

96